Your Guide to Buying Your First Home in Delaware

By: John R. Thomas

Delaware's Number One Mortgage Lender and Certified Mortgage Planner

Your Guide to Buying Your First Home in Delaware

Second Edition

For information contact John R. Thomas at
DelawareMortgages@yahoo.com

ISBN: 978-0-557-34982-1

FIRST EDITION – March 2010

SECOND EDITION – August 2011

Your Guide to Buying Your First Home in Delaware

Table of Contents

Acknowledgments

I would like to thank my wife Bernadette Thomas and my children Max and Madeline for being the inspiration for all that I do. This book could not have been completed without you in my life inspiring me to finish.

I also would like to thank Tim Davis for coaching me to write this book and to get it done. Sometimes all it takes is one person to hold us accountable for reaching our goals and dreams.

I want to thank the people who took the time to review my book and offer their valuable advice on my final edit; Linda Tascione, Lakeisha Cunningham, Douglas MacGray, and Paula Reeves-Carrasquillo.

I would also like to thank Christian David of Nova Models in Baltimore Maryland for doing such a great job on my photographs.

Introduction

The thought of buying your first home is exciting and overwhelming. A home is a great investment for you and your family; in fact the smartest investment you ever make during your lifetime is your home. It provides a place to create memories that last a lifetime. Owning a home changes the course of your life forever. The process of buying a home will help you take control of your money and your credit. It sews the seeds of financial literacy and responsibility. It transforms the way you think about money and wealth if you follow the proper method and take the time to become educated.

Join me on a journey of a lifetime that will not stop once you get the keys to your new home. I am your trusted advisor as leading you through all the steps from start to finish. It doesn't matter where you are right now financially; it matters where you are going. The journey is what is important. It not only is a means to an end so that you can buy your first home: it is an educational process that leads you to so many more opportunities in your life and the lives of the people around you.

Your journey begins by understanding the benefits that homeownership brings. In the words of Steven Covey who wrote *The Seven Habits of Highly Effective People*, you need to start with the end in mind. You need to have a goal and understand all the benefits of that goal in your life.

We will explore together the differences between renting and owning and you will see how dramatic the difference can be on your financial future. Renting is an endless cycle that can keep you trapped paying for someone else's mortgage and building someone else's wealth. Turn the dream of home ownership into a reality by following the simple, step-by-step advice outlined in this book.

Chapter 1

The Benefits of Home Ownership

Why should you buy a home? You should be able to answer this question before you go shopping for a house. You want to know the advantages of buying a home and whether they make sense for you now.

There are five major benefits to buying a home.

1. A Home Is A Sound Financial Investment.

Your home is a sound investment. Why? Your money is safe for the long term *if* you buy the home for a fair price. The risk of your home losing significant value in the short term is minimal, and if you own your home long enough it will almost certainly go up in value. The money you spend on the mortgage payment is a monthly investment towards paying for the house.

2. You Can Stabilize Your Housing Payments

Inflation is one of the key concerns of anyone who is trying to manage their case flow and save for the long term. Your housing cost is one that you can largely freeze and protect from the long-term negative effects of inflation.

You have the ability to take control of your housing payment by getting a 15 or 30 year fixed rate mortgage. This would keep your housing payment fairly stable for the next 15 or 30 years. While homeowners' insurance and taxes may increase, the principal and interest you pay on the loan will stay the same. After the term of the mortgage is over, you essentially no longer have a housing payment. There is no landlord to raise your rent once you buy your own home. If you continue renting you can count on your rent increasing by about 5% per year for as long as your continue to rent.

3. Appreciation of Your Home Will Add to Your Net Worth

When you buy a home you are spending money to take care of a basis need (a roof over your head), but you are also buying an investment. You are investing in real estate. Despite some rare short term decreases, real estate has always increased in value over time. The value of real estate has increased at an average rate of 5-6% over the last 30 years. This increases the equity in your home over time. Equity is the difference between what you could sell your home for and what you owe the bank. For example, if you could sell your home for $200,000 and you owed the bank $150,000 on your mortgage you have $50,000 in equity.

Let's look at how buying a home for $100,000 today can create equity for you over time.

- Purchase home for $100,000 today
- Assume an annual appreciation rate of 5.0%
- After 1 year house is worth $105,000
- After 2 years house is worth $110,250
- After 3 years house is worth $115,762
- After 5 years house is worth $127,628
- After 10 years house is worth $162,889

You can see that after 5 years you have created $27,628 in equity for yourself that you wouldn't have had if you were renting and after 10 years you have $62,889 in equity appreciation.

4. You Control Your Property

Once you buy a home, you take control of the property. You can decide what color to paint your house, what trees to plant, and what other improvements and/or changes to make. There is no landlord to tell you what you can and can't do. There is nothing like having the peace of mind to know that you can now decide what happens to your castle.

5. Owning a Home Provides Tax Benefits

The last major benefit of owning a home is the tax advantages.[1] You can deduct the mortgage interest that you pay every year from your taxable income. You can also deduct the property taxes you pay each year. A tax deduction lowers your taxable income. For example, if you make $45,000 a year in income and you pay $10,000 a year in mortgage interest, you can lower your table income by $10,000. So, you would not have to pay tax on the $45,000 you made, you would only pay tax on $35,000. Now if you also paid $2,000 in property tax, you would lower your taxable income by another $2,000. This would bring your taxable income down to $33,000. So, the difference between renting a home and owning a home in this case is the difference between paying taxes on the $45,000 you made for a renter versus only paying tax on $33,000 of that same income for a home owner. It pays to own a home!

---

[1] The U.S. tax law is quite complex, and you should rely on your tax advisor to inform you as to your specific tax situation. The discussion above is meant to be general in nature and you should not rely on it without obtaining advice from a tax advisor who knows your circumstances. This example also doesn't subtract out your standard deduction.

Chapter 2
Renting Versus Owning

If you are paying rent, you may not be focusing on all the money you are spending on rent each year. You may not be aware of all the benefits you are missing out on because you are renting instead of owning.

Let's look at an example of someone paying $1,500 a month in rent. This would be about what it costs to rent a single family residence in Delaware. We will assume a 5% annual rent increase. After 5 years you would have spent nearly $100,000 on rent!!! What do you get for spending all this money?

If you live in a rented home for 5 years you may fix it up. You might paint, put up some fixtures, etc. When you move out of the apartment, all that money you spent is gone because you don't own the place or any of the improvements you have added. After 5 years, the property value will have increased.

As I illustrated to you in the prior chapter, if you purchased a home at a cost of $100,000 and 5% annual appreciation, after 5 years you, as the owner, would be enjoying a $27,628 in equity gain.

If you are renting that same home, this equity gain is not yours. You don't own the property. So after spending nearly $100,000 you have nothing to show for it.

Anybody want to keep renting?

Here is how the total rent paid was calculated;

Assuming a 5% rent increase per year:

Year	Monthly Rent	Annual Rent
1	$1,500	$18,000
2	$1,575	$18,900
3	$1,654	$19,848
4	$1,737	$20,844
5	$1,824	$21,888

Total $99,480

When someone goes from renting to owning, it usually costs more to own per month than to rent. But that is only for the first couple years. For example, let's say you decide to rent a home for $1,500 a month and your friend decides to buy one with a mortgage payment of $1654 a month. You say you can't afford the extra $154 a month, but the real question is, "How can you not afford to pay the extra $154 a month?"

If you look at the chart above, in 3 years your rent will equal your friend's mortgage payment. In 5 years, you will be paying $170 *more* per month than your friend is paying. Remember, with a 30-year fixed rate mortgage, your payment stays pretty much the same for the next 30 years. So if you couldn't afford the $1,654 a month, how are you going to afford $1,824 a month?

What can you do to afford the higher mortgage payment? Since mortgage interest and property taxes are tax deductible you will have to pay less in taxes than you are currently as a renter. If you do nothing, you will get a refund at the end of the year because you paid too much in taxes during the year. Instead of getting money back the following year when you file your tax return, you can change your withholdings and get the money back each paycheck by paying less in taxes each pay check. This extra money can help you afford a higher mortgage payment.

Let's look at an example of how this might work. Assume Mr. Jones buys a house and gets a $200,000 mortgage at 6.0% fixed for 30 years. He will pay $11,933 in interest in the first year. Let's assume he pays $2,100 a year in property taxes in the first year. His total tax deduction for the first year is $14,033. This means he can lower his taxable income by $14,033 the first year of his mortgage if he itemized his deductions on Schedule A of his personal tax return. When Mr. Jones was renting he paid income tax on the entire gross amount of the income he earned.

How much did Mr. Jones save the first year? The answer depends on which tax bracket Mr. Jones income falls. If we assume it is in the 25% tax bracket, he would have paid 25% of the $14,033 in federal taxes to the IRS when he was renting which is $3,508.25. Now that Mr. Jones owns a home, he can get this money refunded when he files his tax return next year.

If Mr. Jones has no other deductions then he would only save the $14,033 minus the amount of the standard deduction which we will assume is $5,700 for a single filer. So if we subtract the standard deduction ($5,700) from the $14,033 he will be lowering his taxable income by $8,333 which will save him $2,083.25 if he is in the 25% tax bracket.

He can also decide not to pay more taxes than he should by changing his W-4 form with his employer. He will claim more deductions so that he can get this money back every month in his paycheck. If we divide the yearly savings by 12 months, we get $173.60 per month he could be getting in his pay check that is currently being taken out for taxes.

Mr. Jones can use this extra money to help offset the higher cost of a mortgage compared to rent. A good resource to help you figure out your deductions is the IRS website at www.IRS.gov. Enter "withholding calculator" in the search box; the first thing that comes up is the IRS resource for helping you reduce your refund. The IRS cautions that the more accurate information you put in to the calculator, the more accurate the results will be. Here are tips to get the best results:

- Have your most recent pay stubs handy.

- Have your most recent income tax return handy.

- Fill in all information that applies to your situation.

- Estimate values if necessary, remembering that the results can only be as accurate as the input you provide.

- Consult the information links embedded in the program whenever you have a question.

- Print out the final screen that summarizes your input and the results, use it to complete a new Form W-4 (if necessary), and keep it for your records.

Another great resource to help you figure this out is your Human Resource or payroll person at your job. You can also consult with your accountant or tax preparer. A Certified Mortgage Planner can assist you as well.

Let's see how this could help Mr. Jones afford a higher mortgage payment than his current rent. If Mr. Jones is currently paying $1,150 a month in rent for his apartment and a mortgage payment on a home is $1,320 a month for everything including property taxes, home owners insurance, and mortgage insurance that is a $170 increase in his monthly housing expense. If he changes his W-4 form with his employer to receive his tax savings in his pay check, he would be getting an extra $173.60 every month.

If Mr. Jones used this money for his mortgage payment, he is now effectively paying less a month to own a home than he was to rent a home because: 1) his monthly payment only increased by $170 a month and 2) he is getting an extra $173.60 a month in his paycheck! So Mr. Jones is actually saving $3.60 a month by paying the $1,320 mortgage versus the $1,150 rent. This means he is paying less to own a home versus renting a home.

Chapter 3

Getting Ready to Buy

Do you think you are ready to buy a home? Before you even start shopping for a home prepare yourself by taking the following steps.

Step 1 – Make a Household Budget

Step 2 – Get a Credit Check

Step 3 – Establish an Emergency Fund

Step 4 – Get a Written Financial Plan

Step 5 – Get Pre-approved for a Mortgage

Step 1 – Make a Household Budget

The first and most important step is to create a household budget, which allows you to see how much money is coming in and how much is going out. Your budget will help you determine how much mortgage payment you can *really* afford.

However, the guidelines for loan approval may actually let your borrower more money than you can afford. The guidelines look at your debt to income ratio by comparing your gross income to your new housing expense and only the bills you have that are listed on your credit report. This doesn't seem like it is such a big deal at first, but if you think about it, how many people get to take home all of their gross pay? Gross pay is the amount before it is taxed. Also, how many people have more monthly bills than are listed only on their credit report? Most people have more bills not on their credit report than on their credit report.

A budget will look at all your bills and use your income that you actually take home not your gross income. The budget will tell you what you can really afford. This will help you answer the most important question of all: Can you afford the mortgage payment?

A budget has two parts income and expenses. The idea is to keep your expenses below your income. Creating a budget can be simple if you follow these steps:

How to Create a Budget

Step 1 – Write down all your income on a monthly basis

Step 2 – List all your expenses as monthly amounts

Step 3 – Add up all your expenses

Step 4 – If you expenses are more than your income, you need to cut back on your monthly expenses.

Step 5 – Compare your expenses to the ideal

> Housing – 35%
>
> Transportation – 20%
>
> Debt Budget – 15%
>
> All other expenses – 20%
>
> Savings – 10%

Step 6 – Maintain Records & Track your budget

This is typically one of the most difficult or unattractive things for prospective homeowners to do. However, if you get a good handle on this now, it will not only help you determine how much house you can afford, it will help you for the rest of your life to only purchase those things you can afford. This in turn will keep you out of all sorts of unpleasantness for the rest of your life. You can download a **Free Budgeting Worksheet** at www.DelawareFirstTimeHomeBuyerBook.com/Budgeting

Step 2 – Get a Credit Check

The next step is to get a credit check. It is extremely important that you check your credit immediately because repairing bad credit takes time to fix. If you have insufficient credit, it takes time to establish credit. You need to get a tri-merge credit report that provides your three FICO scores in one report from the three major credit bureaus; Transunion, Experian, and Equifax.

If you find errors on your credit report, it usually takes at least 30-45 days to fix anything with the credit bureaus because request must be done in writing. If you find you don't have sufficient credit, it will take time to build it. If you need a plan to help you repair your credit, you should seek a mortgage planner that has a "Get Mortgage Ready Program.". This program will give you a step-by-step plan to repair your credit and get you ready to qualify for a mortgage. You can find information on this program at www.DelawareFirstTimeHomeBuyerBook.com.

Step 3 – Set up an Emergency Fund

The next step is to setup an emergency fund. An emergency fund is money you save in a short term savings account to be used in emergencies only. If you have nothing saved right now in the bank, your first goal is to save one month's worth of bills in a savings account. How do you know what one month's worth of bills are? You should have done a budget in step one that would tell you your monthly bills.

You should make your savings automatic. You should setup an automatic deposit with your paycheck into a savings account that is not linked to your normal checking account. If it is linked to your checking account, you will be tempted to spend it. I recommend setting up a separate savings account. I recommend something like ING Direct Orange Savings Account. It pays a generous interest rate on your savings. You can't get a debit card so you won't be tempted to impulse spend.

Step 4- Write Your Financial Plan

The last step is to make a written financial plan. There is a famous saying "If you fail to plan then you are planning to fail." You must establish financial goals that you want to obtain then design a written plan for obtaining those goals.

Below is a simple financial plan that anybody can use to achieve financial success. It is called the **6 Step Cash Flow Priority Plan.**

6 Step Cash Flow Priority Plan

Step 1 – *Detail Your Short & Long Term Financial Goals*

Step 2 – *Develop a Budget & Analysis Your Cash Flow*

Step 3 – *Establish an Emergency Fund*

Step 4 – *Eliminate Unhealthy Debt*

Step 5 – *Save for Financial Goals*

Step 6 – *Get Proper Insurance to Protect Your Family*

The first step is accomplished by taking out a piece of paper and brainstorming what you would like to accomplish financially in the next 1-5 years. Then organize this list into time frames of when you want to accomplish them. Break it down into goals you would like to accomplish in the next year, next 1-3 years, and next 3-5 years. This gives you your short-term, medium-term, and long-term financial goals.

Once you have organized your goals, you want to write out a plan for accomplishing each goal. The plan would simply be a list of steps that you must take in order to complete the goal. Since you are reading this book, I assume one of your goals is to buy your first home. So you would list the steps that you need to accomplish in order to buy your first home. You would take out a piece of paper and put your Goal at the top: "I Buy My First Home Six Months From Now." Then you would list your steps in order.

Goal – I buy my first home 6 months from now.

Step 1 – I get a credit check within the next 3 days.

Step 2 – I complete a household budget within the next 5 days.

Step 3 – I apply to be pre-approved for a mortgage in the next 5 days.

Step 4 – I save up enough money for my deposit and closing costs within the next 4 months.

Step 5 – I correct any errors on my credit report within the next 3 months.

Step 6 – I meet with a realtor and define where and what type of house I am looking for within the next month.

Step 7 – I start touring homes and actively looking for a home as soon as I have my down payment & closing costs saved up in the bank.

Step 8 – I make an offer on a property within 5 months.

Step 9 – I make settlement on my new home within the next 6 months.

The next step of the financial plan is to develop a budget that analyzes your income and your expenses. A budget is a guide for how to manage your money on a monthly basis. The budget will help you see your monthly cash flow. Cash flow is how your money comes in (income) and how it goes out (expenses). You need to be making more money than you spend so that you will have a positive cash flow.

Step 3 of your financial plan is to establish an emergency fund. The emergency fund is best if it is kept in a savings account that is completely separate from your checking account. This prevents you from being tempted to spend the money. It is to easy to see that new pair of shoes and think I will buy them now with the money in my emergency fund and just put the money back later. Do you really ever put the money back?

Your emergency fund should be a minimum of 1 month worth of bills before you try to do anything else. Then you should work to get it up to at least 3 months of bills. This is important because if you have long-term disability insurance, it doesn't kick in for 90 days, so you need to be able to pay your bills for the first 3 months of your disability. If you lose your job, you have at least 3 months to find a new one until your money runs out. If you speak with a financial planner, they will want you to eventually get 6 months of bills in a savings account.

Step 4 is to put together a plan to pay off your unhealthy debt. This is money that you borrowed to buy "stuff" that didn't make you any money. This is typically credit card debit. You want to have a plan to pay off this debt.

Step 5 of your financial plan is to start saving for your goals. You shouldn't start saving for your financial goals until you have done your budget, created your emergency fund, and started your plan to eliminate your bad debt.

The last step, Step 6, of your financial plan is the most important because if you build some financial security you can lose it all in an instant without the proper insurance protection. You need to make sure you have the proper coverage for home and auto. You should get them with the same carrier so that you can get an umbrella policy that is a personal liability rider that protects you for both home and auto if you injure somebody. You also need to consider the proper life insurance to protect your family. You need to look at disability insurance and long term care insurance for anybody in their late forties to fifties.

Now that you have gotten your financial house in order you are ready to start the home buying process by applying with a mortgage lender to be pre-approved for a mortgage.

Step 5 –Getting Pre-approved for a Mortgage

The last step you should take in getting yourself ready to a buy a home is to get pre-approved for a mortgage from a mortgage banker or broker. A pre-approval will tell you if you qualify for a loan to buy a home. It will tell you how much money the bank will lend you, how much down payment and/or closing costs you will have to pay, and most importantly, how much your monthly mortgage payment will be.

This information is very important so that you don't go out and fall in love with a house that is $250,000 and then find out you are only approved for $200,000. You will not find any houses you like for $200,000 because in your mind you will be comparing all the houses you are looking at to the $250,000 house you fell in love with.

Chapter 4

The Pre-Approval Process

Just like not all banks are created equally, not all pre-approvals are created equally. A true pre-approval should consist of all of the following steps:

Pre-Approval Process

Step 1 – Credit Check

Step 2 – Complete Loan Application

Step 3 – Income Verified

Step 4 – Assets Verified

Step 5 – Loan Guidelines Checked

Step 1 - The Credit Check

What does a lender look for in a loan application? First item any bank will review is your credit report. You must meet minimum credit score requirements and you must not have any items on your credit report that would prevent you from getting a mortgage such as unpaid judgments, unpaid tax liens, default on any federal debt, or unpaid child support. Banks want to know if you pay your bills on time.

A lender will get what is called a tri-merge credit report to verify information that is contained by the three major credit bureaus: Equifax, Experian, and Transunion. The report will show your FICO score from each of the three bureaus. Banks will use your middle score for qualifying you for a mortgage.

Let's look at an example. Let's say your credit report is checked and your scores look like this;

Equifax – 645

Experian – 678

Transunion – 634

You would be a 645 for qualifying purposes. The bank will throw out your top score and your bottom score.

Sometimes you only have two scores because one of the bureaus doesn't have sufficient information to generate a score. In that case, your qualifying score is taken as the *lower* of the two scores. There are almost no loan programs left for anyone with no credit score or only one credit score.

The minimum score to obtain a loan is 620 and some banks have raised it to 640. If your score is at or above the minimum score, the lender will look at the report itself to determine if you have enough credit to qualify.

You typically need 3 tradelines that have been reporting for at least 12 months. A tradeline is an item of credit that is reporting on your credit report such as a credit card or a car loan. If you don't meet the minimum tradeline requirement you can get alternate tradelines added to your credit report. Alternate tradelines are bills that you are regularly paying that are in your name but not reporting to the credit bureaus. Examples of alternate tradelines are cell phone bills, car insurance bills, utility bills, rental payments, etc.

These alternate tradelines are added to your credit report in what is called a "credit supplement." This supplement is just for the purpose of qualifying for the mortgage and is not added to your credit file with the three bureaus.

Your rental history is the biggest clue concerning whether you will pay a mortgage on time or not. Your rental history is typically required to be verified for the last 12 months. Rent can be verified by presenting your last 12 months of canceled checks showing rent paid on time or the lender can do a verification of rent with your landlord which is commonly called by its abbreviation (VOR). For most loan programs, the VOR must be from a property management company not from a private individual. Some loan programs for first-time home buyers will allow private VOR or no rent verification (if, for example, the prospective home buyer is living rent free with family), but your approval will probably not be as high as an approval where they could verify your paying rent.

If you would like to receive a **Free** copy of your **Credit Report**, visit www.DelawareFirstTimeHomeBuyerBook.com/Credit.

Step 2 - The Complete Loan Application

Once you have passed the credit check, your certified mortgage planner will take a complete loan application. It is important that you provide as much information as possible so that your mortgage planner can get a complete picture of your financial situation. The information gathered at the loan application is a lot of detailed, personal information required by the bank and the federal government in order to apply for a home loan.

The mortgage planner must get a complete picture of your residency history and your employment history for the past 2 years. Any gaps in employment or residency must be explained. You will need to provide the complete name, social security number, and date of birth, for each person listed on the loan application.

You will need to provide information on your income. The mortgage planner will need to know if you are paid hourly, salaried, commissioned, or if you are self employed. All of your income will need to be addressed. You will need to provide information on your landlord and who can verify your residency history.

The mortgage planner will also ask you detailed information on your assets. You need to disclose any money that you have even if you don't plan on using it to buy the home. Money that you have that you don't use to buy the home is called reserves. The more money you have in reserve, the more likely your loan application will be approved.

At the time of application, you will need to prove your identity by providing a photo ID. This is very important to protect against identity theft. Once the loan officer takes a complete loan application, he/she will need to verify all the information that you provided.

If you would like to apply for a mortgage to buy a home in Delaware visit www.PRMIDelaware/loanapplication.

Step 3 - Verifying Your Income

The second big thing lenders look at is your income. They want to know whether you have steady income currently and a history of steady income for the past two years. Banks lend money on your ability to make payments every month.

Lenders must compare your gross income to your liabilities; this calculation is called your Debt to Income Ratio

(DTI). There are two ratios your lender calculates, the top and the bottom. The top ratio is a comparison of your gross income to your new mortgage. The bottom ratio is a comparison of your gross income to your mortgage payment and your liabilities on your credit report.

Your employment and income must be verified for the past two years. If you are a W-2 wage earner, you will need to provide your most recent month's worth of pay stubs. If you are bi-weekly, that will most likely be 3 most recent pay stubs. If you are paid semi-monthly, you will need to provide 2 most recent pay stubs. You are also required to provide your W-2 forms for the past two years.

If you haven't worked at the same job for the past 2 years, you will need to provide a detailed list of your past employers with dates worked, names of employers, addresses, and phone numbers. You don't need to provide copies of your tax returns unless you claim un-reimbursed employee expenses on your tax return. These are expenses you incurred while doing your job for which your employer doesn't reimburse you. Lenders must lower your qualifying income by the amount of expenses you claimed on your tax return and you will need to provide a year-to-date list of expenses you are planning to claim on your tax return.

If you are self employed, you will need to provide the last two years of tax returns for your individual filing and your business filing if you had one. You income is calculated by averaging your adjusted gross income for the past two years. The adjusted gross income is what you claimed you made on your taxes after you expensed out all of your business expenses. So you brought in $65,000 as a self employed plumber and claimed $25,000 in expenses for your plumbing business: your adjusted gross income would be $40,000. In this case, you would have to be qualified on $40,000 a year, not $65,000. You will also be - required to provide a year-to-date Profit & Loss statement (P&L). For most loan programs, you must have been self employed for at least 2 years before the self-employment income will qualify you for a mortgage.

You can have a second job and use that income to qualify only if you have had a history of a second job for the past 2 years. If you receive overtime or bonuses, you can use this income as qualifying income as long as you have received it for the past two years and your employer will verify it is "likely" to continue. Overtime and bonuses are averaged over the last two years.

A verification of employment from your employer is also required as part of verifying income. A verbal verification of employment is required to be repeated within 24 hours of the closing to ensure that the borrower is still employed. If your employment status cannot be verified, the closing will be delayed or the loan may even be denied. This is now required because some people have quit their jobs days before settlement and the lender didn't find out until after the loan closed. The Bank is lending the money on your ability to pay the money back every month which is only guaranteed by your current employment.

You must have a 2-year history of steady employment. If you have changed jobs in the same field or to make more money, that is not looked at unfavorably. If you have changed from one job to another and haven't kept a steady job, you will probably be denied a loan until you have been at your current job for at least 1 year to ensure that you won't continue job hopping with no permanency.

If you were in school to get a degree or learn a trade, the schooling will count as employment history as long as you get a job in the same field as your degree. Therefore, if you went to college to get a degree as a registered nurse and just graduated 4 months ago and are now working as an RN at a hospital, you would qualify with using your school as part of your 2 year work history. You will be required to provide either a school transcript or a diploma.

Other sources of income include Social Security, disability, pensions, child support and alimony. All these income sources can be used as long as you can prove they will continue for at least 3 years and you can show proof you have received them for the past 3 months.

Step 4 - Verifying Your Asset

Assets are any source of funds that you have available to you. This can be money in any of the following;

- Checking Accounts
- Savings Accounts
- CDs
- Money Market Accounts
- Retirement Accounts
- Brokerage Accounts (Stocks & Bonds)

The assets you listed on your loan application must be verified and your mortgage planner must also verify you have enough money to cover your down payment and your closing costs.

Banks are required by law to verify all money that is in a bank account to be properly sourced. This means CASH is BAD!!! Lenders cannot work with un-sourced funds from a borrower. Banks are required to verify any account by reviewing the 2 most recent statements for any accounts listed on the loan application. When reviewing the statements every deposit no matter how small must be verified as to the source of the deposit. Cash deposits into an account that cannot be sourced cannot be used and can taint the whole account so that none of the money in that account can be used for the purchase of the home.

If your practice is to cash your pay check, pay your bills with the cash, and deposit the left over money into the bank, STOP! Deposit your check into your bank and take out only what cash you need so that you don't have any cash deposits going into your bank account.

When a lender is reviewing your bank statements, if there are charges for non-sufficient funds (NSF) to cover ATM withdrawals or checks you wrote on the account, your loan could be denied. NSF fees on a bank account are a red flag indicating to a potential mortgage lender that you can't manage your money and routinely spend more than you make. A bank is not going to lend you money if you have numerous NSF fees on your account. If you had one or two and it can be explained in a letter that is signed by the borrower that might be okay.

You can get a gift from a family member, employer, or close personal friend to help with down payment or closing costs. But this can only be done if the person giving the gift can provide proof they had the money in a bank account before they gave it. The donor needs to provide a bank statement that shows the money and no large deposits. If there are large deposits in that account before the gift was given, those deposits must be sourced or the gift will not be allowed. You are not allowed to receive CASH gifts to help with down payment or closing costs. In addition to a bank statement from the donor showing the money to give, you will also need to provide proof the gift was given which is a copy of the check and you must provide proof the gift has been deposited into your account. The proof the gift has been deposited is simply a bank statement showing the deposit.

The 401K for Down Payment!

Most 401k accounts and 403b accounts have an option when you can borrower money without any penalties or taxes. The withdraw is a loan against the account so you will be charged interest, but the best part, you pay the interest to yourself! This is often a much better option than the first time home buyer programs for down payment assistance because almost all of them charge interest but you are paying the interest to the government. Who would you rather pay interest to, yourself or the government?

Retirement accounts require that the most recent quarterly statement be provided and if account is not being used for down payment or closing costs but being used as reserves, and only 60% of the value of the account is used for reserve. If you are pulling money out of a retirement account for the purchase of the home, you must provide a statement before you pulled the money out showing you had the money available. You must provide a copy of the check or money transfer and finally a copy of your bank statement showing the funds have been deposited.

It is important to list all funds available to you on a loan application because money that you don't use will be counted as a reserve. Reserves are money you have left over after you buy the home. This is very important for loan approval. Banks like to see that you don't spend every dime you have to buy a house. Some other sources of reserves or source of funds are life insurance policies that have a cash value, cars, jewelry, etc. In order to use items such as cars or jewelry as reserves, the items must be sold and the money deposited into your bank account.

The last step to complete a pre-approval is for the mortgage planner to review the loan guidelines for your particular loan program. This ensures that your loan application meets all the loan guidelines and won't be denied in underwriting because there is something in the loan guidelines that would disqualify your application.

It is very important your pre-approval states what loan program is being used. A pre-approval without a specific loan program may mean that your loan application wasn't reviewed under any loan guidelines. This could mean you might not qualify once the loan program is picked and the loan is underwritten.

Once all of these steps have been completed you should have a Good Faith Estimate that clearly lays out how much your estimated monthly payment will be and approximately how much money you will need for down payment and closing costs. You should also receive a pre-approval letter which states the maximum purchase price you qualify for and what loan program you are using. The pre-approval letter should also state if you need any seller assistance with closing costs. Your pre-approval should also include the interest rate that was used to qualify you. This is important because if rates go up you may no longer qualify for that loan amount.

If you receive a pre-approval letter and the loan officer or mortgage planner didn't collect all of your income documentation and asset documentation you are not really pre-approved. This is very important because there are still lots of bad loan officers who do not do a complete pre-approval and cost many home buyers thousands of dollars a year because they enter into a sales contract and end up having their loan denied when the income and asset documentation is finally reviewed.

Delaware Closing Costs for a Purchase Transaction

When you apply for a loan you will be given a Good Faith Estimate of the closing costs and a truth in lending form which will show your annual percentage rate (APR). The closing costs vary from state to state and even from county to county in a particular state.

Common closing costs in Delaware are as follows;

The Lender Fees;

Appraisal Fee – Fee paid to the appraiser to determine the fair market value of the property. $450

Processing Fee – Fee paid to cover the cost of processing the loan. Usually includes covering the fees for obtaining credit reports, tax transcripts $499 - $599

Underwriting Fee –Fee charged by the lender to cover the cost of underwriting the loan and administrative costs. $599 - $899

Flood Certification Fee – Fee charged to obtain flood certification certificate. $9-$19

Discount Points – Points charged to buy your interest rate down to a lower rate. (1%-2% of the loan amount)

Loan Origination Fee – A fee charged for doing your loan or fee charged because of bad credit score. (0.5%-2% of the loan amount)

Pre-Paid Interest – You will pay a per diem interest from the day you close till the end of the month.

* Note – As of January 1, 2010 the GFE has changed so that all the lender fees are lumped together as loan origination fee, the fees are broken out on an itemized fee sheet or loan summary.

The Attorney & Title Fees;

Attorney Fee – Fee charged by the attorney for his services. ($300 - $500)

Title Search – Fee charged to search the title of the property. ($110-$160)

Title Insurance – Fee charged to purchase owners and lenders title insurance ($3.83 per thousand of purchase price)

Title Insurance Binder – Fee charged to put the title report together and prepare the closing protection letter. ($25-$30)

Wire Fee – Fee charged to accept the incoming wire from the lender ($10-$15)

Overnight Fee – Fee charged to overnight the loan package backed to the lender ($40-$50)

Government Fees;

Recording Fee – The County will charge you to record your deed and your mortgage. The County charges per page. ($250-$364)

Transfer Fee – The state of Delaware charges a 3% transfer that is split equally between the buyer and the seller. The buyer will pay 1.5% which is split between the State and the County. The County gives first time home buyers an exemption on the transfer tax so you are only responsible to pay the state portion which is 0.75% of the purchase price.

Pre-Paid Items;

Hazard Insurance Premium – This is your first year's homeowner's insurance premium that will be paid at closing. ($300-$850)
Survey – The fee paid to have the property surveyed, the fee changes based on the County. ($250-$650)

Home Inspection – Fee paid to the home inspector to inspect the property. ($350-$450)

Pest Inspection – Fee paid to have the property inspected for wood destroying insects. ($55-$85)

Escrow Account – You will be required to let the lender pay your property taxes and hazard insurance, so they will need to collect money to setup your initial escrow account.

Seller Reimbursements;

Pre-paid property taxes – $ varies based on property

Pre-paid County Sewer bill - $ varies based on property

Pre-paid HOA fee - $ varies based on property

All of these closing costs should be disclosed to you on a Good Faith Estimate (GFE). The Good Faith Estimate **NO LONGER** will provide you with your estimated *monthly payment* or the estimated *cash needed* to close!!! The Federal Reserve decided to "simplify" the GFE by making a one page document 3 pages and removing the two most important pieces of information: your payment and the cash you need to close.

Your lender should provide you with a loan summary or an itemized fee sheet that shows your estimated payment and the cash you need to close. You should also receive a Truth in Lending (TIL) form with your GFE. The TIL will show your annual percentage rate (APR). The APR is not your real interest rate. The APR shows your note rate plus the finance charges over the term of the loan.

On the next page is a copy of the 3 pages of the new GFE that is required to be used on loan applications taken on or after January 1, 2010:

Page 1 & 2 of GFE

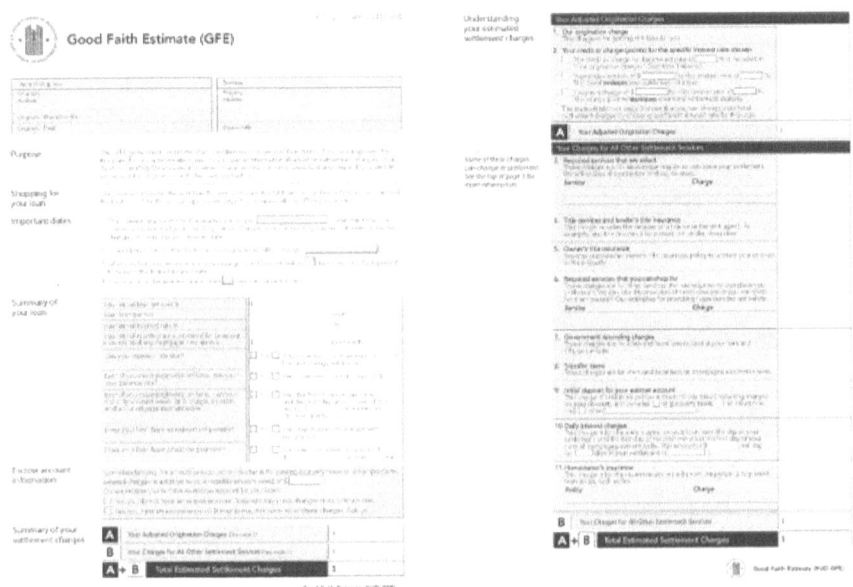

Page 3 of GFE

Chapter 5

Understanding Credit

One of the first things a lender does when you apply for a mortgage is to check your credit report. The lender will order a credit report from each of the three main bureaus; Equifax, Transunion, and Experian. The lender receives one credit report with a combination of all three reports in one credit report. This type of report is a called a Tri-Merge Credit Report. It is ordered through a credit reseller which charges lenders money to get a copy of each report from the individual bureaus and then pull it all together into one report which is sent to the lender. The tri-merge report will display all three FICO scores and what information each of the three bureaus are reporting.

What is a credit score? A credit score is a 3 digit number used by lenders to evaluate the risk associated with lending you money. The score is generated by a mathematical model created by Fair Isaac & Company in the 1950s which is termed your FICO score.

What does your credit score mean? The score represents the statistical chance of the borrower going 90 days late over the next 24 months. The scores range from 300 to 850, the higher the score the better and the lower the score the worse.

What do you need in order to generate a credit score? You must have an account that is at least 6 months old, have been updated in the last 6 months, and not be in dispute. Without this, you will have no score and no credit is the same as bad credit.

Your credit score is generated by looking at Five Factors; Payment History, Balances Carried, Credit History, Mix of Accounts, & Inquiries. The five factors are not weighted equally.

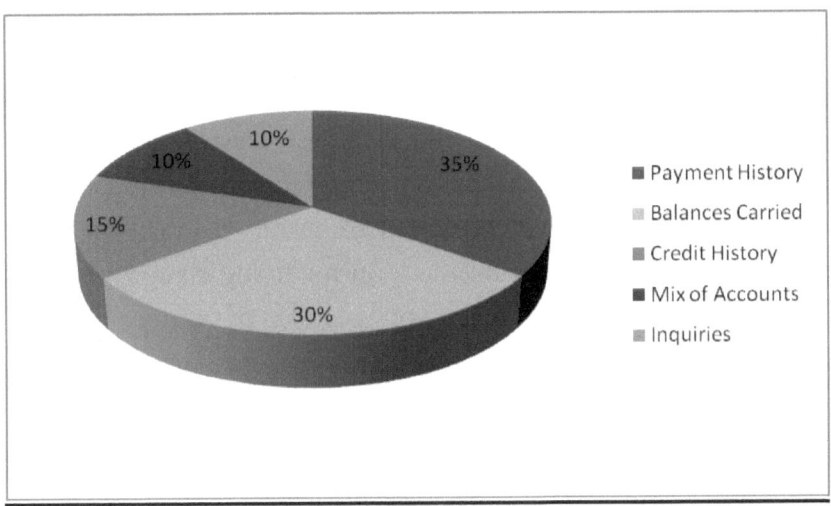

The breakdown is as follows;

> Payment History – 35%
>
> Balances Carried – 30%
>
> Credit History – 15%
>
> Mix of Accounts – 10%
>
> Inquiries – 10%

Payment History – This category looks at how you have paid your bills that are listed on your credit report. Paying your debt on time and in full has the greatest positive impact on your credit score. Negative items such as late payments, judgments, collections, charge offs, past dues, and tax liens all have a negative impact on your credit score. The last two years have more effect than older items.

Paying past due current will give the greatest boost in score for this category. If trying to improve your credit score, you need to make sure you don't pay anything 30 days or more late. If you do, you will erase any boost in your score that you might have worked to get.

Balances Carried – This is the second largest factor that affects your credit score. It compares the ratio between your available credit and how much of that credit you are using. You get the most points for keeping your balances on revolving charges under 30%. You lose points when you use 50% of your available limit. You lose more points when you are using 80% of your available limit and lose even more when you max it out at 100%.

Credit History – Credit History is a measure of how long a credit line has been open. The longer you have had an account the more points you will get for this category. You get an initial bump when you open a new account. The next bump is at 6 months and then again at 12 months. You should never close an account because you will lose points for the credit history of that line now that it is closed.

Mix of Accounts – This category looks at the mix of credit you have. The more varied your credit types the better your score will be in this category. You should carry 3-5 credit cards with balances less than 30% of the limit or zero. The ideal mixture according to FICO is 1 mortgage, 1 car loan, and 3-5 credit cards.

Inquiries – This category looks at the number of hard inquiries on a credit report over the last 12 months. A hard inquiry is and inquiry you have made to try to obtain credit such as for a mortgage or a car loan. The inquiry can cost you between 2 and 25 points.

How do you establish credit if you have no credit? You will need to apply for a secured credit card. A secured credit is a card where you send the credit card company $300 and they will give you a credit card with a $300 limit. It is called secured because they already have your money. I recommend getting two secured cards to build your credit because you will need at least 3 tradelines to qualify for a mortgage. You will need one other tradeline such as a cell phone, utility, car insurance, rent, etc.

You will need to be very conscious of how you use the credit card. You need to keep the balance below 30% of the limit so that you get the most points for that credit card. If you limit is $300, you need to keep the balance at $89 or less. Here is website for a secured credit card **http://budurl.com/securedcredit**. This card reports to all three credit bureaus.

The most important thing to build good credit is to pay all your bills on time! Another way to build good credit is to get a secured loan from a credit union or bank that will allow you to deposit $1,000 into account and then borrower a $1,000 against your own money. It is a secured loan because you have already provided the bank with the money that you will be borrowing. It is important that you ask in advance if bank will report to all three bureaus. This is important so that you can build credit with each bureau.

Your credit score is used by lenders to determine which mortgage programs you may apply for. You score is also used to determine your base interest rate. This is termed "risked based pricing". Risk based pricing means that the lower your credit scores, the higher your rate will be. For the most part, you cannot get a mortgage without having a credit score.

For more information on Credit Scores, you can download a **Free Credit Scoring Handbook** at www.DelawareFirstTimeHomeBuyerBook.com/Credit.

Chapter 6

Credit Repair

How do you increase your credit score?

If you have bad credit and need to increase your credit score and clean up your credit report, you need to follow these steps;

Step 1 – Pay all past due accounts current.

Step 2 – Pay all bills on time from now on.

Step 3 – Pay down balances on revolving charge cards below 50% if possible.

Step 4 – Keep unused accounts open.

Step 5 – Write dispute letters disputing collection accounts, charge offs, judgments, and late payments. Negative accounts that have not recently reported are more likely to be deleted in a dispute.

Step 6 – Settle recent collections that cannot be deleted in a dispute. Try to get creditor to provide letter stating account should be deleted.

When you write dispute letters to the credit bureau they must investigate and resolve issue within 30 days. Don't dispute on www.annualcreditreport.com, bureaus get 45 days to investigate instead of 30 days. Sample dispute letters are provided in the appendix. When disputing items with the credit bureaus, you must provide photo ID to prove your identity and proof of address with some type of bill that is sent to your address such as utility bill. If you don't provide this information, bureau will ignore your request and state that you need to prove your identity and verify your address before they will investigate your dispute.

When a consumer disputes the accuracy of an item contained in a file from a bureau, the Fair Credit Reporting Act (FCRA) requires that the bureau:

- Reinvestigate free of charge, record the current status of the disputed information or delete it
- If dispute is determined to be frivolous or irrelevant the consumer is notified in 5 business days from the date determined.
- Include the reason for the determination and any information needed to reinvestigate the dispute.
- Notify the consumer in 5 business days of the results of the reinvestigation.

You can still get added as an authorized user to boost your credit score as of this writing but the new scoring model called FICO 08 removes the authorized user account from the scoring model. The credit bureaus have not instituted FICO 08 yet for mortgage credit reports so an authorized user account can boost your credit score. It will not be counted as one of your required tradelines. You want to find someone with a credit card that has a balance below 30% and is always current and has at least 24 months of credit history, the longer the better.

For Free Copies of **Credit Dispute Letters** to send to the credit bureaus visit www.DelawareFirstTimeHomeBuyerBook.com/Credit.

Chapter 7

Understanding Mortgages

There used to be hundreds if not thousands of different loan programs available in the market. Most of these loan programs disappeared in 2007 when the mortgage market collapsed. The vast array of loan products termed "Subprime loans" disappeared along with stated income and state asset programs. Your exotic adjustable rate products such as option ARMS disappeared and so did the dreaded pre-payment penalty. The 100% financing on conventional loan products vanished along with the 80/20 program. The 80/20 was a way to buy a home with a 100% financing by getting a first mortgage for 80% of the value of the home and a 2nd mortgage for the other 20% of the value of the home.

The mortgage products available today for consumers are in two categories only; conventional loan programs and government loan programs. Within these two programs you can choose a fixed rate mortgage or an adjustable rate mortgage termed an ARM. A fixed rate mortgage means the rate is fixed for the life of the loan. For example if you purchase a home with a 5.5% 30 year fixed rate mortgage, your rate will stay 5.5% for the full 30 years so your principle and interest payment will be the same for the full 30 years. An adjustable rate mortgage is fixed for a certain number of months or years and then will change after that period. For example if you get a 5.25% 5 year ARM for 30 years, your interest rate of 5.25% is fixed for the first 5 years of the 30 year loan. After the first 5 years the interest can adjust either up or down depending on the current market conditions. For more information on adjustable rate mortgages, see Appendix A – Understanding ARMs

You can also choose the term of your loan which is called the amortization period. You can choose between a 30 year, 20 year, 15 year, and a 10 year term. Gone are the 50 year and 40 year mortgage products that became popular at the height of the mortgage craze in 2006.

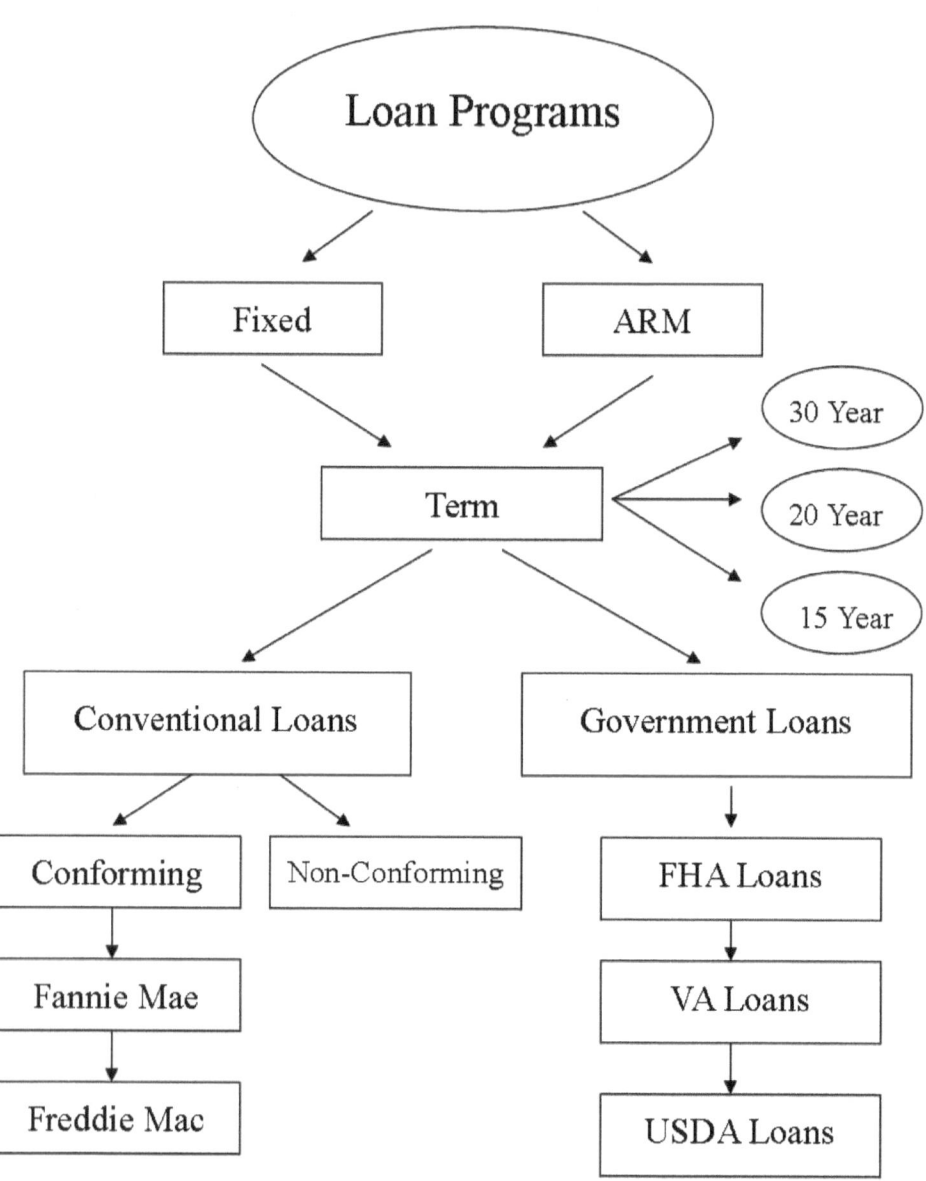

What is a conventional loan program?

A conventional loan is a loan that is made by a lender or a bank and either serviced by that bank or sold on the secondary market. Most conventional loans are conforming loans which means they must follow the guidelines setup by Fannie Mae and Freddie Mac. The conforming loan limits for Delaware are $417,000. Conventional loans now require a minimum down payment of at least 10%. Any conventional loan over 80% requires Private Mortgage Insurance (PMI). PMI is insurance paid for by the borrower that insures the lender against default by the borrower on the mortgage. In order to qualify for the mortgage insurance you must have very good credit and low debt to income ratios.

Currently Conventional loans must follow the Home Valuation Code of Conduct (HVCC) law that came into effect on May 1, 2009. The law restricts how appraisals are to be done. The Appraisal must be ordered through an appraisal management company. This law has made appraisals more expensive for the consumer. It has made appraised values come in lower and has caused the process to take at least twice as long. It also prevents mortgage brokers or bankers from estimating your value before hand to determine if it makes sense to do a refinance.

What is a Government loan? Government loans are loans that are still made by banks but are insured by the government against default of the borrower on the mortgage. This means if the borrower stops paying the mortgage and the bank has to foreclose on the property, the government agency will buy the property from the bank because it insured the loan.

There are three types of government insured loans; FHA Loans, VA Loans, and USDA Rural Housing Loans. FHA loans are loans insured by the Federal Housing Authority. This type of loan is currently the most used loan among first time home buyers. VA loans are loans insured by the Veterans Administration. USDA Rural Housing loans are insured by the Rural Development Agency.

What is an FHA Mortgage Loan?

In 1965 the Department of Housing and Urban Development (HUD) was formed. Within HUD operates the Federal Housing Administration (FHA), which has the primary responsibility for administering the government home loan insurance program. This program is completely funded by the borrowers who use the program and no tax payer dollars are needed to support the program. FHA loans allow a first time home buyer who might otherwise not qualify for a home loan to obtain one because the risk is removed from the lender by FHA who insures the loan for the lender.

The most popular FHA home loan program for a first time home buyer is by far is the 203(b). This is your standard fixed rate loan for 1-4 family owner occupied houses and only requires a minimum of 3.5% from the borrower as a down payment. This loan also permits 100% of their money needed for down payment and closing costs to be a gift from a relative, non-profit organization, or government agency.

There are two main advantages to a FHA home loan. The first is that the credit criteria for a first time borrower are not as strict as Conventional Loans sold to Fannie Mae (FNMA) or Freddie Mac (FHLMC). Someone who may have had a few credit problems or little traditional credit should not have a problem obtaining FHA financing. The second advantage is the down payment requirement is much less (3.5% versus 10-20%) Also, FHA home loans are assumable, allowing a person to take over the mortgage without the additional cost of obtaining a new loan.

- FHA only requires the borrower to put down 3.5% of the purchase price as down payment.
- FHA has no minimum credit scores but most banks require minimum 640 or higher.
- FHA will allow the seller to pay up to 6% of the closing costs & Pre-paid items.
- FHA requires you to pay monthly mortgage insurance.
- FHA will allow you to have a non-occupying co-borrower.
- FHA has no income limits.
- FHA will allow gift funds for down payment & closing costs.
- FHA has no reserve requirements.
- FHA is limited to owner occupied properties only
- FHA will allow borrower to borrower funds from approved sources (secured)
- FHA loans have no pre-payment penalties
- FHA loans are assumable.

The eligible borrowers for FHA loans are US Citizens, Permanent Resident Aliens, Non-permanent Resident Aliens, and non-occupant co-borrowers. All borrowers must have valid social security numbers in order to qualify for FHA loans. Credit Requirements require that all judgments, tax liens, and past due child support must be paid before borrower can qualify for loan.

FHA loans have appraisal requirements that require the appraiser to determine if the property is safe, structurally sound, and to determine the value of the property. The appraiser will need to visual inspect roof and look for peeling paint on properties built before 1978 because of lead based paint issues. If the FHA appraiser determines there are any issues with the property he will require repairs to be made. Once repairs are made, appraiser will go back out to property to verify the repairs have been completed.

FHA loans also have anti property flipping rules. FHA requires the owner to have owned the property for at least 90 days. The sales contract cannot be dated for less than 91 days after the owner purchased the property or it will not qualify for FHA financing. If there is less than 180 days of ownership, two appraisals may be required by the lender.

FHA has loan limits are based on the county in which the property is located. In Delaware there are three counties; New Castle County, Kent County, & Sussex County. The loan limits for 2010 and 2011 are as follows;

New Castle County - $420,000

Kent County - $376,250

Sussex County - $376,250

The maximum loan limit is before the upfront mortgage insurance is added onto the loan. FHA currently charges 1.0% of the loan amount in upfront mortgage insurance on a loan used to purchase a home. The insurance is added to the loan amount. For example if you are buying a house in New Castle County, Delaware, you can get a max loan of $420,000. The upfront mortgage insurance premium is $4,200 so when we add this to the base loan amount of $420,000 we get a total loan amount of $424,200.

The Qualifying Debt to Income (DTI) ratios for an FHA loan are 31/43. This means that 31% of your gross income can be used for your housing expense and 43% of your gross income can be used for your housing expense and all other credit liabilities. You can be approved for higher ratios if you have compensating factors such as current rent equal to the new mortgage payment and three month or more of reserves. For example if you make $3,000 a month in gross income and your new housing payment will be $930 per month, your top ratio is 31%. If your housing and other expenses combined are $1,290 per month then your top number is 41%.

What is a FHA 203k Loan?

The FHA 203k loan is a rehabilitation loan used to purchase and repair a property all in one loan. When a homebuyer wants to purchase a house in need of repair or modernization, the homebuyer usually has to obtain financing first to purchase the dwelling; additional financing to do the rehabilitation construction; and a permanent mortgage when the work is completed to pay off the interim loans with a permanent mortgage. Often the interim financing (the acquisition and construction loans) involves relatively high interest rates and short amortization periods.

The FHA 203k loan program was designed to address this situation. The borrower can get just one mortgage loan, at a long-term fixed (or adjustable) rate, to finance both the acquisition and the rehabilitation of the property. To provide funds for the rehabilitation, the mortgage amount is based on the projected value of the property with the work completed, taking into account the cost of the work.

To minimize the risk to the mortgage lender, the mortgage loan is eligible for endorsement by HUD as soon as the mortgage proceeds are disbursed and a rehabilitation escrow account is established. At this point the lender has a fully-insured mortgage loan which takes much of the risk away to the lender on a rehabilitation loan.

There are two versions of the FHA 203k loan, the full version and the streamline version. The streamline version is much easier for the borrower and for the lender so is the loan of choice when possible.

The process for a 203k rehab loan is as follows

Step 1 – **Home Buyer Locates Property**

Step 2 – **Preliminary Feasibility Analysis** - After the property is located, the homebuyer and their real estate professional should make a comparable market analysis prior to signing the sales contract. The following should be determined:

> 1) The extent of the rehabilitation work required;
>
> 2) Rough cost estimate of the work; and
>
> 3) The expected market value of the property after completion of the work. Note: The borrower does not want to spend money for appraisals and repair specifications (plans), then discover that the value of the property will be less than the purchase price (or existing indebtedness), plus the cost of improvements.

Step 3 – **Sales Contract is Executed** - A provision should be included in the sales contract that the buyer has applied for Section 203(k) financing, and that the contract is contingent upon loan approval and buyer's acceptance of additional required improvements as determined by HUD or the lender

Step 4 - **Homebuyer Prepares Work Write-up and Cost Estimate.** A consultant can help the buyer prepare the exhibits to speed up the loan process.

Step 5 - **Lender Requests HUD Case Number.** Upon acceptance of the architectural exhibits, the lender requests the assignment of a HUD case number, the plan reviewer, appraiser, and the inspector.

Step 6 - **Fee Consultant Visits Property.** The homebuyer and contractor (where applicable) meet with the fee consultant to ensure that the architectural exhibits are acceptable and that all program requirements have been properly shown on the exhibits.

Step 7- **Appraiser Performs the Appraisal.**

Step 8 - **Lender Reviews the Application** The appraisal is reviewed to determine the maximum insurable mortgage amount for the property

Step 9 - **Issuance of Conditional Commitment/Statement of Appraised Value.** This is issued by the lender and establishes the maximum insurable mortgage amount for the property.

Step 10 - **Lender Prepares Firm Commitment Application.** The borrower provides information for the lender to request a credit report, verifications of employment and deposits, and any other source documents needed to establish the ability of the borrower to repay the mortgage.

Step 11 - **Lender Issues Firm Commitment.** If the application is found acceptable, the firm commitment is issued to the borrower. It states the maximum mortgage amount that HUD will insure for the borrower and the property.

Step 12 - **Mortgage Loan Closing.** After issuance of the firm commitment, the lender prepares for the closing of the mortgage. This includes the preparation of the Rehabilitation Loan Agreement. The Agreement is executed by the borrower and the lender in order to establish the conditions under which the lender will release funds from the Rehabilitation Escrow Account. Following closing, the borrower is required to begin making mortgage payments on the entire principal amount for the mortgage, including the amount in the Rehabilitation Escrow Account that has not yet been disbursed.

Step 13 - **Mortgage Insurance Endorsement.** Following loan closing, the lender submits copies of the mortgage documents to the HUD office for mortgage insurance endorsement. HUD reviews the submission and, if found acceptable, issues a Mortgage Insurance Certificate to the lender.

Step 14 - **Rehabilitation Construction Begins.** At loan closing, the mortgage proceeds will be disbursed to pay off the seller of the existing property and the Rehabilitation Escrow Account will be established. Construction may begin. The homeowner has up to six (6) months to complete the work depending on the extent of work to be completed. (Lenders may require less than six months.)

Step 15 - **Releases from Rehabilitation Escrow Account.** As construction progresses, funds are released after the work is inspected by a HUD-approved inspector. A maximum of four draw inspections plus a final inspection are allowed. The inspector reviews the Draw Request (form HUD-9746-A) that is prepared by the borrower and contractor. If the cost of rehabilitation exceeds $10,000, additional draw inspections are authorized provided the lender and borrower agree in writing and the number of draw inspections is shown on form HUD-92700, 203(k) Maximum Mortgage Worksheet.

Step 16 - **Completion of Work/Final Inspection.** When all work is complete according to the approved architectural exhibits and change orders, the borrower provides a letter indicating that all work is satisfactorily complete and ready for final inspection. If the HUD-approved inspector agrees, the final draw may be released, minus the required 10 percent holdback. If there is unused contingency funds or mortgage payment reserves in the Account, the lender must apply the funds toward the balance of the mortgage principal.

For more information on FHA 203k Loans please visit www.DelawareFHA203kLoans.com

What is a VA Home Loan?

VA loans are loans that are offered by banks but are backed by the United States Veterans Administration. This guarantee allows the banks to still offer 100% financing to qualifying participates. The program began in 1944 after President Franklin D. Roosevelt signed the Servicemen's Readjustment Act of 1944, also known as the GI Bill of Rights. Although the program has been adjusted several times since 1944, the purpose remains the same: To ensure that US veterans can secure a long-term loan for a home.

Prospective candidates for VA loans must meet the military service requirements set forth by the VA. The requirements depend on when you served, how long you served and how you were discharged. To determine if you are eligible for a VA loan, it is best to look on-line at the Veteran's Administration website: www.va.gov. The guidelines are listed under the "Home Loan" benefit section and clearly outline who is eligible to obtain VA financing. Qualifying candidates include Retired US Veterans with certificate of eligibility, active duty with proof of military service, unmarried surviving spouse of veteran deceased from service related death.

Eligible Branches of Service

- Army
- Air Force
- Marine Corps
- Navy
- Coast Guard
- Public Health Service
- National Oceanic and Atmospheric Administration

Highlights of VA Loans

- No Monthly Mortgage Insurance
- No Down Payment Required for loans of $417,000 or less
- Will lend a maximum of $1,000,000
- Allowed to finance VA funding fee into the loan
- No Pre-payment penalties
- Lower Closing Costs than Conventional Loans
- Seller Can pay up to 4% in closing costs or pre-paid items
- Very Competitive Interest Rates

The VA loan maximum limit is $417,000 for a no-money-down loan on a single-family home, but additional jumbo amounts are available to qualified borrowers up to $1,000,000.

Jumbo loan rules:

- A 25% down payment is required for any amount over $417,000.
- You are required to pay the funding fee up front.
- Your credit score must be 680+ if the loan amount is above $650,000 and sufficient debt-to-income ratio to determine what amount you are approved to borrow.
- Other restrictions may apply.

There are many uses for a VA home loan, including:

- Buying a home, condominium, or townhouse.
- Building a new home.

- Buying and improving a home at the same time.
- Installing energy efficient improvements to a home.
- Refinancing an existing VA loan to get a better interest rate.

The VA Loan Funding Fee is required by law and varies according to the type of loan, military service status, and other factors. A first-time VA home loan borrower with a no-money-down loan currently pays an amount equal to 2.15% of the loan. This amount is subject to change depending on legislation and other factors. Some borrowers are exempt from the funding fee:

- Veterans on VA compensation for service-related disabilities.
- Veterans who would receive compensation for service-related disabilities if they didn't draw retirement pay.
- Surviving spouses of military members who died in service or from service-related disabilities.

When necessary, the VA reserves the right to make final exemption determination on a case-by-case basis.

VA determines your eligibility and, if qualified, a certificate of eligibility (COE) will be issued. Your lender will need this document in order to provide you with a VA Loan. You may be able to request a certificate of eligibility through your lender. In some cases, however, you may have to request a certificate by sending in a request for the certificate of eligibility (and any required supporting evidence) to an eligibility center. Under "normal" circumstances, you should receive a response within 10 days. Because this time may vary, it is strongly recommended that you allow your lender to order (ACE) - Automated Certificate of Eligibility. When you receive your

COE you will get an entitlement amount of $36,000. This is full entitlement amount and doesn't mean you are limited to only a loan of $36,000. You are still able to borrower a 100% up to $417,000.

VA Loans require the appraisal to be ordered by the bank through the VA online website. The VA then assigns the appraisal request to a VA approved appraiser. The property must meet VA appraisal guidelines or a list of required repairs will be called for by the appraiser. Once the required repairs have been completed, the appraiser re-inspects the property to confirm the repairs are satisfactory.

The appraisal is used by VA or a VA approved underwriter to issue a Notice of Value (NOV). The notice of value establishes the value for the property and may or may not be the value assigned by the appraiser.

VA also establishes a procedure for interested parties to dispute the NOV or the appraised value. The interested party would write a letter disputing the NOV and provide the comparable sales that they feel support a different value. VA would then review the file and issue a final NOV.

For more information on Delaware Veteran Loans please visit www.Delaware-VA-Loans.com

What is the USDA Rural Housing Loan Program?

Rural Housing Service (RHS) was created in 1994 as a result of the Department of Agriculture Reorganization Act to meet housing and community development needs of rural America. Section 502 Rural Housing Guaranteed Loans are loans made by private lenders such as banks but are guaranteed by the Rural Housing Service. This means if the borrower defaults on the mortgage, Rural Housing Service will pay the bank back for the loan.

Rural Housing Service (RHA) is part of Rural Development (RD) in the US Department of Agriculture (USDA). The local Rural Development servicing Delaware is located in Dover, DE.

There is no required down payment, but families must be able to afford the mortgage payments, including taxes and insurance. In addition, applicants must be without adequate housing and be unable to obtain credit elsewhere, yet have acceptable credit histories. Since there are no other options currently for 100% financing it is easy to show borrower is unable to obtain credit elsewhere.

Highlights of USDA Rural Housing Program
- No Monthly Mortgage Insurance
- No down payment required
- 103.5% financing based on the appraised value
- Seller can pay closing costs and pre-paid items
- Income restrictions based on number of people in household

- Gifts for closing costs permitted
- No Reserves Required
- No minimum Credit Scores
- Geographical Restrictions on qualifying properties

The income guidelines for debt-to-income ratios for USDA Rural Development loans is 31/43. This means 31% of your gross income can be used for your total housing payment and 43% of your gross income can be used for your total expenses. You can exceed the ratio guidelines by asking for a ratio waiver but you must have a minimum 620 credit score and must have other compensating factors. Compensating factors include at least three months of reserves and rent payment equal to new housing payment.

The income guidelines for how much you can make depend on the county where the subject property is located. The income guidelines are as follows;

New Castle County Maximum Income Limits for 2011

1 - 4 Person	5 - 8 Person
$0 - $90,050	$0 - $118,850

Kent County & Sussex County Maximum Income Limits for 2011

1 - 4 Person	5 - 8 Person
$0 - $74,050	$0 - $97,750

The geographical restrictions are displayed below in the maps for each of the three counties in Delaware. The dark areas are not eligible for USDA rural housing loans.

Legend
○ Cities
⚡ Major Interstates
⚡ Interstates and Highways
⚡ Other Major Roads
☐ Counties
▨ Lakes and Rivers
▨ SFH Ineligible Areas
☐ States

New Castle County Delaware

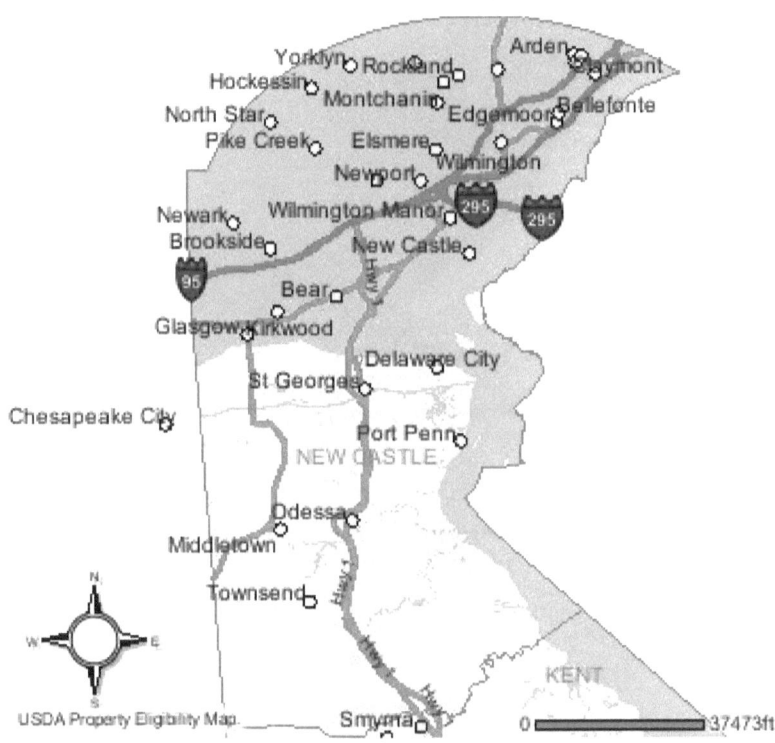

Kent County Delaware

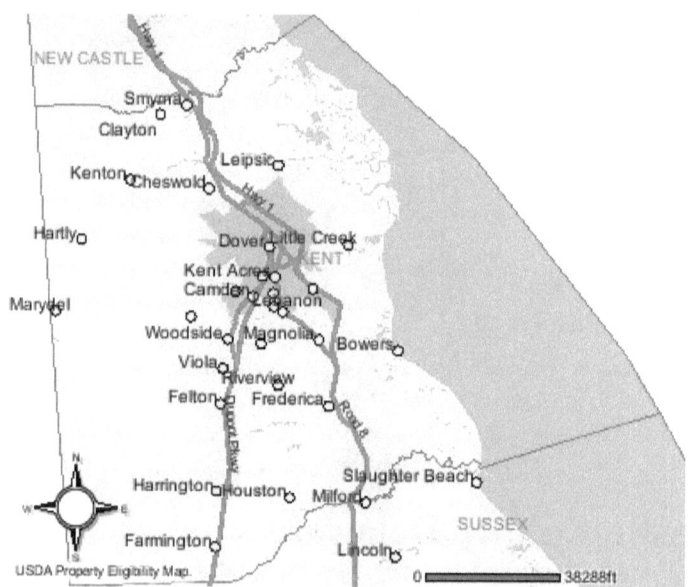

Sussex County Delaware

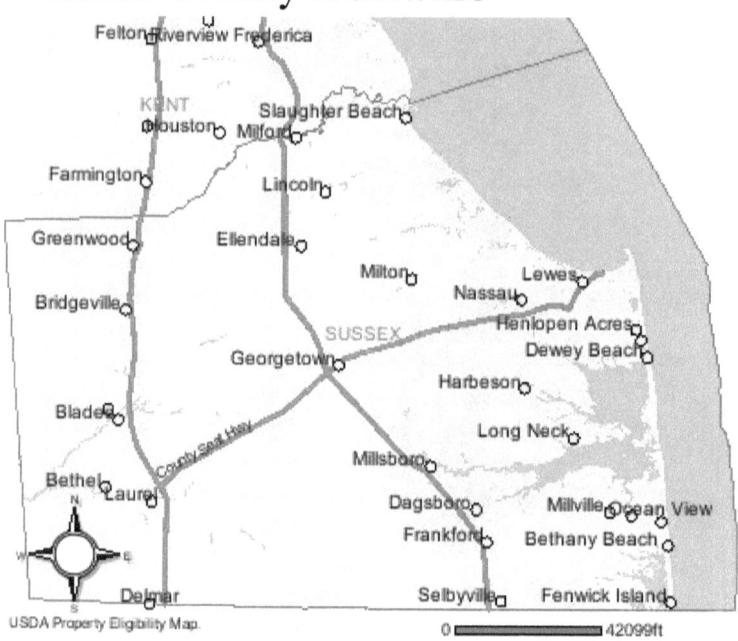

You can check if a property is in a RD eligible area – Visit the following website and put in the street address - http://eligibility.sc.egov.usda.gov

Your mortgage payment will consist of the principal, interest, property taxes, and home owner's insurance. The principal portion of your payment is the part that goes to paying back the money you borrowed. The interest portion is the monthly interest charged based on the remaining principal amount. The property taxes and home owner's insurance are paid once a year by your lender so your lender divides the yearly amount by 12 and adds this to your monthly mortgage payment. When the money is collected each month it is put into an escrow account until the bill comes and then the lender pays the bill from the escrow account.

What affects your interest rate?

Trying to find the best rate is almost impossible because interest rates change every day and sometimes two to three times in the same day. The reason the interest rate changes nearly every day has to do with the fact that the rate is tied to the mortgage backed security bond that is traded daily on the open market. When the market is selling the mortgage bonds the interest rate goes up when the market is buying the mortgage bonds the interest rate goes down.

So if you call one bank in the morning and get a rate quote of 5.25% and call another bank in the afternoon and get a rate quote of 5.125% you may think the second bank has the better rate. But what might have happened is the bond market improved and mortgage rates re-priced for the better in the middle of the day. So the second bank you called may have the same rate as the first or maybe even slightly worse if the bank you called in the morning re-priced to 5.0%. Most banks have the same rate within a 0.25%. So it is more important to find a mortgage planner you can work with that you trust and can provide you the education and service you need versus searching all over town for the lowest rate.

The following factors all affect your interest rate so without knowing all these factors you interest rate quote is not accurate;

Credit Score	Loan to Value	Pre-Paid Points
Loan Program	Occupancy	Rate Lock Period
Fixed vs. Adjustable	Rental Payment History	
Size of the Loan	Amortization Period	

Your interest rate quote is only good till you get off the phone with your lender because rates can change anytime the market is open and bonds are being traded. You can't lock your rate till you have a property and a signed sales contract.

What is a Subprime Mortgage?

A subprime mortgage is a loan made to a borrower who would not normally qualify for a loan, perhaps due to bad credit issues or other financial problems. Subprime lenders charge borrowers higher interest rates for potential losses the lender might incur.

The subprime mortgages are blamed for the high rate of foreclosures that lead to the Recession of 2008 & 2009. The Subprime mortgage market all but disappeared in 2008 & 2009. The lenders have all disappeared and the government enacted legislation that made most of the loans that were originated as subprime loans illegal now.

What is Mortgage Insurance?

Mortgage insurance is insurance that is paid for to protect the lender when a borrower goes into default and the lender must foreclose on the property. The mortgage insurance does not protect the home owner. It insured the lender against some of the loss when a home owner goes into default for not making the mortgage payments.

Why do lenders require mortgage insurance? Lenders require mortgage insurance in order to take the risk when loaning money that is more than 80% of the value of the home or there exists an inherent risk in the loan type such as FHA.

Without mortgage insurance and government guarantee fees, borrowers would be very limited on the mortgage products available. There would only be loans available that required borrowers to make at least a 20% down payment.

The mortgage insurance is different depending on which type of loan is used. For example conventional loans have several options for mortgage insurance and charge different amounts depending on the down payment. Loans with LTVs of greater than 80% but less than 85% have the least expensive mortgage insurance. The next bracket is 85% to 90%, then 90% to 95%. The higher the LTV on conventional loans the stricter are the requirements for qualifying for the mortgage insurance.

Conventional loans give the borrower the option of paying the mortgage insurance monthly or paying a onetime fee upfront and removing the monthly fee. There is also the option of lender paid mortgage insurance which allows the lender to pay for the mortgage insurance premium by increasing the interest rate on the loan.

FHA loans charge a onetime upfront mortgage insurance premium of 1% of the loan amount which can be financed into the loan. FHA also charges a yearly mortgage insurance premium that is charged monthly as part of the monthly mortgage payment. The calculation of the monthly mortgage payment depends on two things, the loan-to-value and the term of the loan.

FHA can change the upfront and the monthly mortgage insurance but the current as of April 18, 2011 is as follows:

30 Year Mortgages:

LTV greater than 95% is calculated using 1.15%

LTV less than 95% is calculated using 1.10%

15 Year Mortgages:

LTV greater than 90% is calculated using 0.50%

LTV less than 90% is calculated using 0.25%

USDA Rural housing loans currently have no monthly mortgage insurance but have a 3.5% upfront guarantee fee. This is 3.5% of the loan amount and is allowed to be financed into the loan. In October of 2011 the upfront fee is being lowered to 1% and they are adding monthly mortgage insurance for the first time. It will be calculated using 0.30%.

Veteran Loans (VA) do not have monthly mortgage insurance but do charge an upfront funding fee that can be financed into the loan. The fee is 2.15% of the loan amount for the first time usage.

Chapter 8

Shopping for a Home in Delaware

The steps to follow for shopping for a home are as follows:

Step 1 - *Select your team of professionals*

Step 2 - *Interview with your Buyer's Agent*

Step 3 - *The Search*

Step 4 – *Making the Offer*

Step 5 – *Offer Accepted*

Step 1 - Selecting Your Team of Professionals

Once you have been pre-approved for a mortgage to buy a home you are ready to go shopping. Your pre-approval will have your maximum purchase price and how much seller assistance you will need. You will use this information to determine the price range of homes you should be searching. You will need to begin identifying who will be on your real estate team. Your real estate team will consist of the following people:

The Lender (Certified Mortgage Planner)

Real Estate Agent (Buyer's Agent!!)

The Attorney

The Home Inspector

The Appraiser

The Home Owners Insurance Agent

The Home Counselor

Selecting your lender is probably the most important decision in the whole home buying process. You need to make sure your loan consultant is licensed as a loan originator by the State of Delaware. The Federal Government passed legislation called Secure and Fair Enforcement for Mortgage Licensing Act of 2008 (SAFE Act) to require all mortgage originators to be licensed by taking an initial 20 hour pre-licensing course then passing a national licensing exam along with any state exams. Applicants must also submit to criminal background checks as well as credit checks.

The Federal banking agencies have exempted employees of federally regulated banks such as Wells Fargo, Bank of America, etc. This means the loan officers at these big banks don't have to be licensed and don't have any educational requirements, background requirements, or credit requirements! So you might want to consider how much the loan officer at a big bank really knows and whether he is even qualified to advise you on your financial decisions.

Be sure to ask the loan officer your are working with for their license number for the state of Delaware. You should also select a loan consultant that is a certified mortgage planner (CMP) or a certified mortgage planning specialist (CMPS) so that they can not only advise you on the best loan product but can help you with budgeting, credit repair, tax implications of your mortgage, and help you manage your mortgage after the transaction is complete.

When you discuss being pre-approved your loan officer should provide you with a loan summary and take the time to explain all the charges and fees that you will be paying. Make sure they are doing your Loan Summary as worst case scenario not best case. You want to make sure you will be able to afford the mortgage payment and will have enough money to cover closing costs. If you get worse case scenario then you know you will be okay. If your pre-approval is based on best case then you may be in for a shock when the rate you get is higher and the closing costs are higher. The only people offering you best case scenario is someone who is trying to win your business by presenting an unrealistic scenario and is not looking out for your best interest.

Before January 1, 2010 we provided prospective clients Good Faith Estimates that provided the information above but the US government changed the law and we are no longer allowed to provide a GFE until the time of an application which is now defined by the borrower having a sales contract. So you should now receive something called a loan summary to help you understand your payment and costs before you make an offer on a property.

Selecting Your Real Estate Agent

The next person you need to pick is a real estate agent. In Delaware an agent can represent the seller, the buyer, or both according to the law. It is very important that you never call the name on the sign for a house listed for sale, that person works for the seller. They are called the "Listing Agent". You need to get your own Buyer's Agent to represent you. If you call the Listing Agent they will tell you they can work for you, which is true but they are already under contract working for the seller. Their job is to sell the house for as much as they can. They also have another motive for working with you and the seller; they get to keep the whole commission.

In Delaware the seller pays the commission for the listing agent and the buyer's agent. If you as the buyer don't come with your own agent, then the listing agent gets to keep the full commission. For Example, if Jane Smith lists her house for sale with Joe from Real Estate Company X and agrees to list for a 6% commission then it would be paid 3% to the listing agent and 3% to the buyer's agent. Without you brining your own agent, the listing agent gets to keep the full 6% commission. So the seller in essence pays your buyer's agent to get you a great deal.

Selecting the right Real Estate Agent to be your Buyer's Agent is extremely important. You want someone who specializes in working with First Time Home Buyers. You want a full time real estate agent that knows the local market and has sold homes in the county you are looking to buy. The Real Estate Agent will work very closely with you from the initial search all the way up to you getting your keys to your new house. Feel free to contact me and I can recommend some top agents in all three counties of Delaware that specialize in First Time Home Buyers.

If you need to get a recommendation for one of the top real estate agents that work exclusively with First Time Home Buyers visit www.DelawareFirstTimeHomeBuyerBook.com/realtors to see a list of the best Real Estate Agents in Delaware by county.

Selecting Your Real Estate Attorney

The next person that you want to select is your real estate attorney. Delaware law requires you to use an attorney to represent you in the real estate transaction. You want to select an attorney that is a full time real estate attorney. If you were brought up on murder charges you wouldn't get a bankruptcy attorney to defend you. You would want to get the best defense attorney that specializes in getting people off for murder. So you want an attorney that specializes in Delaware Real Estate Law.

It is important to know which attorney you will be using when you first start looking for a home because you may need their advice on any unique situations that come up when writing an offer to purchase a home. You also want to make sure you don't get pressured into using the attorney that the seller wants to pick. It is not the seller's choice; it is your choice because the attorney is representing you in the transaction. When you are looking at new construction, do not let the builder force you into using their attorney. Their attorney has the builder's best interest at heart not yours! The attorney fees and title fees are always considerably higher than if you got your own attorney. A good buyer's agent will negotiate for you not to have to use the builder's attorney.

Selecting Your Home Inspector

The next person on your team will be the home inspector. You want to make sure you pick an ASHI certified home inspector. You should seek referrals from your real estate agent because they should be attending all the home inspections. This allows them to know the good ones from the bad ones. Your home inspector will also perform your pest inspection and radon test in most cases. The home inspector should offer you not only a home inspection report but also a future home maintenance guide.

If you need a recommendation for a great home inspector visit www.DelawareFirstTimeHomeBuyerBook.com/inspectors.

Selecting Your Appraiser

The next person on your team is the appraiser. The appraiser works for the bank and his job is to inspect the property for the bank to determine the value of the home and to determine if the condition of the home meets the guidelines for whatever loan program you are using. As of May 1, 2009 for a conventional loan and as of February 15, 2010 on an FHA loan your mortgage planner can no longer select the appraiser. The appraisal must be order by a third party company called an appraisal management company. The appraisal management company will then assign the appraisal to an appraiser. So you and your lender no longer have any control over who appraises the property.

Selecting Your Homeowners Insurance Agent

The next person on your team is your homeowner's insurance agent. You are required by the lender to purchase homeowners insurance on the property. It is best to start with whoever has your current auto insurance. You will get a group discount if you have your home and auto with the same insurance company. As soon as you get a contract on a house you need to contact your insurance agent to get a quote for the homeowners insurance.

Selecting Your Home Counselor

The last person on your team is the housing counselor. If you use one of the first time home buyer programs in Delaware you are required to take 8 hours of home counseling from a HUD approved counselor. There are several different agencies in Delaware to choose from. For a complete list of home counseling agencies go to

www.DelawareFirstTimeHomeBuyerBook.com/homecounselor

Step 2 – The Interview with your Buyer's Agent

The first thing your real estate agent will do is schedule an interview before they show you any properties. Your agent will review your pre-approval letter to determine what the maximum purchase price is for prospective homes to show you. The pre-approval letter will also let them know if they need to ask for seller paid closing costs. The pre-approval will determine the terms your agent puts in your purchase agreement offer.

During the interview your real estate agent will ask questions to help you decide what the most important features are for your new home. Most people start with location. Everybody says in real estate, it is all about location. Delaware is divided into three counties; New Castle County, Kent County, and Sussex County. You start by narrowing your search down into which county you would like to live. Once you narrow the county down you need to answer the following questions

1) Do you need to be in a specific school district?
2) Do you need to be close to a job or a daycare?
3) If you are willing to travel some distance to work, you may be able to find a home for less money.

These questions help you and the realtor narrow your location down. The next thing you need to get clear on is the features you need and the ones you want in the home. You will generate a list of needs and a separate list of wants. Try to estimate your needs for at least the next 5 years.

1) How many bedrooms do you need?
2) How many bathrooms do you need?
3) Do you need a garage?
4) Do you need a single family home or will a townhouse work?

Step 3 – The Search

Once you and your real estate agent have mapped out where and what you are looking for, the agent will start sending you homes that meet your criteria. Your agent will generate this list of homes from a database of homes called the Multi Listing Service (MLS). The local MLS is called TREND and it covers homes listed in Delaware, Maryland, Pennsylvania, and New Jersey. Every home that is listed for sale in the state of Delaware by a real estate agent is listed on TREND. If you have e-mail, your agent can set you up so that you automatically get e-mailed any new listing that meet your search criteria as soon as the homes are listed on TREND. The MLS is also the source for homes listed on common websites like realtor.com. The difference is the websites don't instantly update so you may be looking at houses that have already sold, whereas if your realtor sends you homes from TREND those are real time and are for sale the moment they are sent.

Once you have found 3-8 homes you would like to see, your agent will setup a tour. The tour will take about 2-3 hours depending on how many homes you select. The agent has to get permission to tour the homes so you need to give your agent advanced notice.

When you are touring a home you are going to be noticing how the home looks and feels to you. Your buying decision is typically emotional and can be influenced by the stuff in the home, the décor, and the color of the paint on the walls. Good Listing agents know this and will even pay to have the home staged with nice furniture and fixtures. This is done to influence your buying decision. Your real estate agent is going to be looking at the house as if there was nothing there. Your agent will be inspecting the property looking for defects and also looking if similar homes that aren't staged or don't have as nice a paint job are priced at a lower price.

Step 4 – Making the Offer

Once you find a home you wish to buy, you make a purchase offer. You already know the maximum amount you can afford, but deciding how much to offer should be based on the following factors:

- What are the average sales prices for homes in the area with similar features and characteristics?
- What condition is the home in, and what repairs or improvements are needed?
- Are similar homes available at a more desirable price?
- How long has the home been on the market?
- Has the sales price already been reduced?
- Is the seller considering other offers at this time?

Your real estate agent will be able to provide you with answers to all these questions. Your real estate agent will also review "The Seller's Disclosure" with you. This is a document that the seller is required by law to fill out if they have lived in the property. This document requires the seller to disclose any known defects with the property. The form is called the "Real Property Condition Report" and can be found on the state of Delaware's website at http://dpr.delaware.gov/boards/realestate/forms.shtml . A seller must complete this form unless one of the following eight exemptions exist;

1. Transfers by a fiduciary in the course of the administration of the decedent's estate, guardianship or trust.
2. Transfers pursuant to court order such as transfers ordered by the Court of Chancery in the administration of an estate, trust or guardianship or pursuant to a Writ of Execution, by a trustee in bankruptcy or a receiver, by eminent domain, and transfers resulting from a decree for specific performance.
3. Transfers to a mortgagee by a mortgagor in default by a deed in lieu of foreclosure.
4. Transfers by any sheriff's sale for default on an obligation secured by a mortgage, judgment, tax or other lien.
5. Transfers from one co-owner to one or more other co-owners.
6. Transfers made to a spouse or to a person or persons in the lineal line of consanguinity of one or more of the transferors.
7. Transfers between spouses resulting from a property settlement incident to a divorce.
8. Transfers to or from any government entity.

Your agent will provide you with a comparative market analysis (CMA). This is an analysis of all the homes that have recently sold, are pending sale, and are currently listed for sale. Using this information, your agent will determine the value of the home you are considering purchasing. This will help you both make a decision as to what you are willing to pay for the house and where you should start you offer price. You realtor will also help you determine how much your earnest money deposit check should be that you submit with your offer. The earnest money deposit is money you present to the seller to show them you are serious about buying the house. If your contract is accepted by the seller, the earnest money check gets deposited into the listing agent's escrow account and the money will be credit towards your closing costs or down payment at settlement.

You may go back and forth as you and the seller counter each other's offer. This is normal and sometimes the outcome depends on how well your real estate agent can negotiate. If you can work out a mutually acceptable contract of sale, then both sides will ratify the contract by signing it. Once this happens you are officially under contract and the earnest money check is deposited. The home should be changed from "For Sale" to "Pending Sale" in the TREND system. This lets all other agents and buyers know that the house is under contract.

In Delaware there is a standard real estate sales contract that all real estate agents use. Your real estate agent should make sure that you are using some important contract contingencies to protect you. The first one is a home inspection contingency. This allows you to have a home inspection done by a licensed inspector. If there are any defects found in the report, your agent will submit an addendum to the contract asking for repairs to be made prior to settlement. The seller can accept the addendum and agree to the repairs, can counter your addendum or refuse to fix anything. If you can't come to an agreement then the contract of sale is terminated and you will receive your deposit money back. If you agree to buy a house "as is" then the home inspection contingency is removed from the contract and you must buy the house no matter what turns up on the inspection report.

If you would like to download a copy of the Delaware Real Estate Sales Contract, visit www.DelawareFirstTimeHomeBuyerBook.com/Realtors.

The second major contingency is the appraisal contingency. This says that the house must appraise for the purchase price or the contract price can be renegotiated. If you and the seller cannot come to terms on a new contract price then the contract is terminated and your deposit will be returned. The last big contingency is the mortgage contingency. This says you must apply for and be approved for a mortgage. If your loan is denied as to no fault of your own, then your contract is terminated and your deposit is returned.

Types of Properties

Single Family Residence (SFR)

Townhouse/Row Home

Twin Homes

Condominium

Mobile Homes

New Constructions

Single Family Residences are typically thought of as homes that are not attached to any other homes, often called Detached Homes. These can be of several different styles; Ranch, Raised Ranch, Split Level, Bi-Level, Colonial and Cape Cod.

Townhouses are attached to one or more homes in a row of houses. You can have an end unit that is on the end and only attached to one other house or you can have an interior unit that is attached on both sides. Townhouses can also have garages on first floor.

Row homes are typically found in the city and have the same characteristics as a townhouse. Row homes have flat roofs where as town homes have gabled roofs.

Condominiums (Condo) can be like apartments or can be townhouses. The difference is when you buy a condo you are buying the unit not the exterior or land. You pay a monthly condo fee for maintenance of common areas and the exterior of your unit. Condos are different in that they must be approved for financing by the lender.

Mobile Homes are homes that used to be a motor vehicle with a VIN number. You take the wheels off and fix it to a foundation. It is extremely tough to get a traditional mortgage on a mobile home. Only double wide mobile homes qualify and they must be fixed to a permanent foundation. You must also own the land, you can't lease the land.

New Construction is fine for first time home buyers if you are having a builder build the house. The home must be completed before you buy it and it must receive a certificate of occupancy. When shopping for a new construction home you will be visiting the building site. The builders will try to convince you not to use a realtor. It is very important that you don't fall for this ploy. They pay your realtors commission and if you don't have a realtor they save money. Without a realtor you will have nobody representing you in the negotiations and if you think you are savvy enough to negotiate against the builder as a first time home buyer you are seriously mistaken and will be taken advantage of by the builder. You must visit the builder with your realtor or disclose that you have a realtor on your first visit and give their name. If you don't the builder will try to get out of paying your realtor their commission and try to get you to drop your realtor.

The builder will try to get you to use their settlement attorney and their lender. It is very important that you don't fall for this ploy. The builder will offer you an incentive to use them but the incentive is usually not real because their lender and settlement attorney will charge very high fees that end up being almost equal to the incentive. If you have a good realtor, they will get the builder to offer the incentive and let you use your own attorney and lender.

There are pros and cons to buying new construction

Pros:

- 10 Year Warranty on the construction of the home

- Warranties on all major appliances and systems

- You get to select the features and color schemes of the home

Cons:

- Large deposits required – typically at least $5,000

- Lot Premiums are charged

- Waiting period for house to be built

- Sometimes no house to see if model hasn't been built

See Appendix F for pictures of home styles on page 133.

Chapter 9

Purchasing a Home in Delaware

Once your contract is accepted, your earnest money check is deposited into the listing agent's broker account and you are officially under contract. You will be required to make official mortgage application typically within 7 days of acceptance of your purchase contract. Here is an overview of the process;

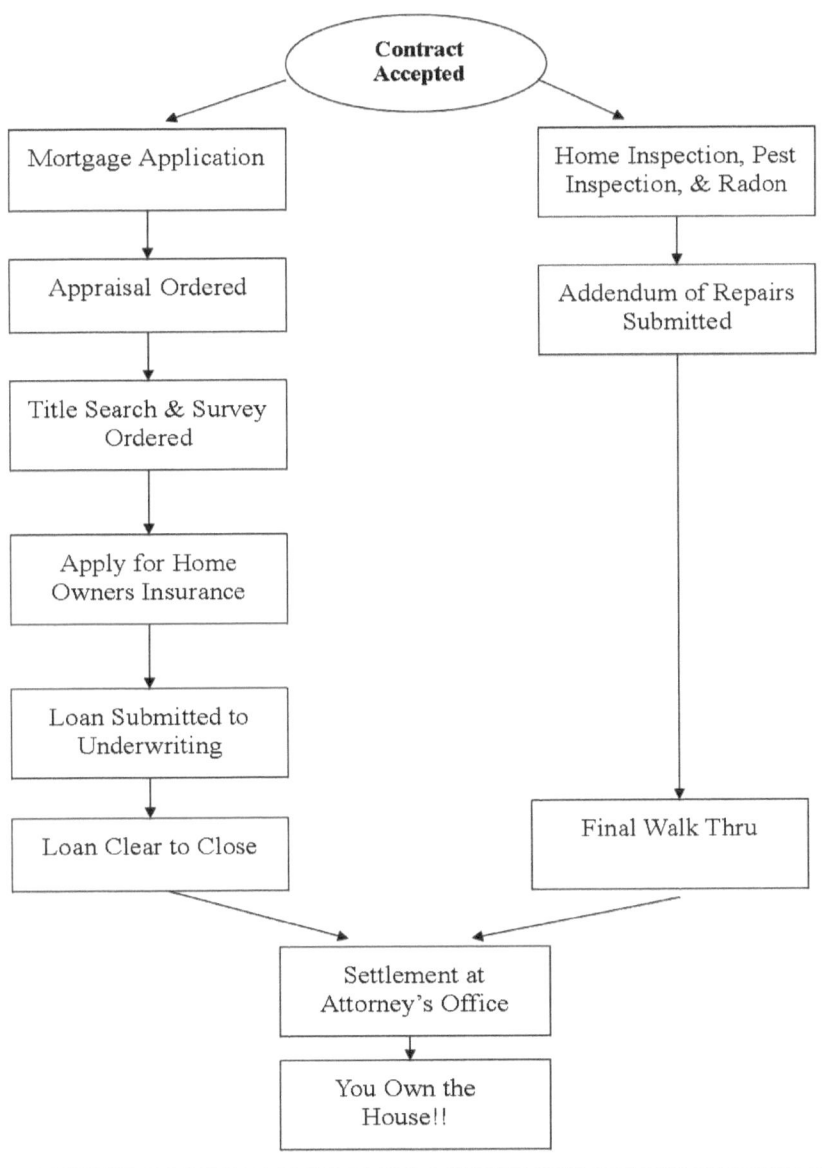

You will meet with your lender within the first 7 days of your sales contract being accepted as required by the contract. You will sign all of the mortgage disclosures, the loan application, Good Faith Estimate, and the Truth in Lending. You will also provide the lender with updated pay stubs, bank statements, and retirement account statements because the ones you presented for pre-approval have probably expired. You won't need a new credit check as long as you will be closing within 90 days of when it was last checked by the lender.

RESPA stands for the Real Estate Settlement Procedures Act which is a law that requires the lender to provide disclosures to the borrower within 3 business days of application. The Two forms you are required to receive are the Good Faith Estimate and the Truth in Lending. The GFE is a summary of the settlement charges and an estimated monthly payment. The Truth in Lending will show you the Annual Percentage Rate (APR). The APR is higher than your note rate and shows you the cost of the credit over the whole term of the loan.

In Delaware the lender is required to have you sign a lock-in agreement form and an itemized schedule of charges form. These are two Delaware required disclosures. The lock-in agreement form should clearly state the interest rate you are getting, whether the rate is lock or not, how long rate is locked for if locked, whether you have loan commitment at the time of signing, and clearly state if you are paying any origination points or discount points. Your lender is also required to provide you with a settlement service provider disclosure which will disclose whose settlement fees they are using on your Good Faith Estimate.

The Appraisal

The appraisal is ordered by the lender to determine the value of the home often termed the "Fair Market Value". The lender wants to make sure the home is worth at least the purchase price or more. This supports using the home as collateral for the loan being applied for by the borrower. The fair market value of a home is determined by having the appraiser use comparable recent sales from similar homes in close proximity to assess the value of the home being purchased by the borrower.

The lender will require the appraiser use comparables that are no more than 6 months old. The lender will also require the appraiser to look at not only recently sold homes, but homes that are pending sale and listed for sale. This is important because the current housing market is declining so lenders want to make sure the value hasn't dropped since the last sale.

The borrower has no choice in the selection of the appraiser and neither does the mortgage planner. For VA loans the appraiser is randomly selected by VA from among local VA approved appraisers. For Conventional loans, the appraiser is selected by an appraisal management company. For FHA loans, starting February 15, 2010 the appraiser will be selected by an appraisal management company. Only USDA loans still allow the appraiser to be selected by the mortgage planner.

You will receive a copy of the appraisal and it is required by law that your lender provide you with a copy. The appraisals are not "portable" any longer, meaning you cannot take an appraisal that was order by one bank and take it to another bank. If you change lenders, the new lender must order their own appraisal.

How Does the Appraiser Assign a Value for the Home?

The appraiser will review 3-4 homes that have recently sold that are similar to the subject property and are within 1 mile radius to the home if possible. The appraiser will look at 4 main features and make adjustments accordingly. The 4 main features are;

- Square Footage of the home & lot
- Appearance
- Amenities
- Condition

What if the property appraises for less than the sales price?

When your appraisal comes in lower than the sales price your lender will use that as the value of the home not the purchase price. When this happens, the lender will reduce your loan amount so that it is based on the maximum loan-to-value for this new lower appraised amount. If your purchase contract had an appraisal contingency then you can take one of these actions;

- Walk away from the deal
- Negotiate with the seller to lower the purchase price
- Put down more money to make up the difference between purchase price and appraised value
- Dispute the appraisal by supplying additional comparable sales that support a higher purchase price.

The Inspections

You real estate agent will put several inspection contingencies into the sales contract so that you can determine if there exist any defects with the house that you were not aware of. The inspection contingency can call for a home inspection, a pest inspection, a radon test, well test, septic test and a lead paint inspection. The contract will have a date for when the inspection must be performed by and when the addendum must be delivered to the seller for any requested repairs. Failure to make the date means that you cannot ask the seller to make any repairs and you are still under contract to buy the house. So it is very important that you get your inspections scheduled ASAP. It is also important that your real estate agent draws up the addendum requesting repairs to be made and deliver it to the seller before the required date per the contract. If your real estate agent fails to deliver the addendum on time, you are still responsible because your agent works for you.

Home Inspection

A home inspection is an objective visual examination of the physical structure and systems of a house, from the roof to the foundation. The standard home inspector's report will cover the condition of the home's heating system, central air conditions system (temperature permitting), interior plumbing and electrical systems; the roof, attic and visible insulation; walls, ceilings, floors, windows and doors; the foundation, basement and structural components.

The home inspection should be done by a certified home inspector. It is recommended that you use an ASHI Certified Home Inspector. Make sure the person that is doing your inspection is ASHI certified not just the owner of the company. You can find an ASHI certified home inspector in your area by visiting their website at http://www.ashi.org/. A good home inspector will not only give you a list of repairs to be made but will also give you a list of maintenance items for your new home. You and your real estate agent should be present at the inspection so that you know what repairs you need to ask the seller to do. Without being present at the inspection, you will not know exactly is wrong and will not be able to effectively communicate to the seller what needs to be repaired.

Once the inspection is completed, you will receive a detailed report on the home. Your realtor will use this report when drafting an addendum asking the seller to make necessary repairs.

Pest Inspection

Almost all of Delaware is subject to infestation from wood-destroying insects and organisms in varying degrees. With few exceptions, the common denominator for this activity is excessive wood-moisture levels. This moisture can be due to roof leaks, plumbing leaks, un-vented crawl spaces and attics, or construction defects such as wood-soil contact. In general older homes are more susceptible to infestation; however, any home is a candidate if conditions are right.

You are required to have a pest inspection if you are getting a government insured loan (VA, FHA, or USDA). The pest inspection will search for any wood destroying insects. It will look for active pests and for damage. If active pests are found during the inspection then the report will call for treatment. Proof of treatment must be provided prior to settlement in order to get the loan cleared. If damage is found then the inspector may call for a contractor to inspect the property to make sure there are no required repairs to be made. If contractor finds damage that needs to be repaired, repairs must be completed before you can make settlement on the home.

The inspector will provide a Wood Destroying Insect Report or WDIR which is not just a termite report. It is the careful examination to the accessible areas of a structure for visible signs of damage from wood destroying insects. It pinpoints special areas of concern such as locations of previous treatment. The report provides valuable information for the sale of a home and documents its present conditions. Some of the commonly noted wood destroying insects are: Carpenter Ants, Carpenter Bees, Powder Post Beetles, Old House Beetles, and Wood Borer Beetles. The WDIR is required to be signed by both the buyer and seller.

Radon Test

Radon is a cancer-causing, radioactive gas. You can't see radon gas and you can't smell. It is essentially an invisible gas. It can be a problem in your home if it builds up in levels that are unsafe. When you breathe air that contains significant amounts of radon, you can get lung cancer. Radon is the second leading cause of lung cancer in the United States according to the Surgeon General.

Radon comes from the breakdown of radioactive material called uranium. The uranium is naturally occurring in rocks, soil, water and "decays" over time into radon gas that will find its way up to the surface because it is less dense than the soil and rocks. Radon is found all over the United States and can get into any building type. Testing for Radon is the only way to know for sure if you and your family are at risk from Radon Gas. Testing is fairly easy and almost all home inspectors will perform the test.

The inspector will leave a test kit behind in the home for 2-3 days to get an accurate reading. This is called a short term test.

The EPA has instituted a Rating system for classifying the risk potential for elevated levels of Radon in counties throughout the US. There are three zone classifications; Zone 1, Zone 2, and Zone 3. Zone 3 has low potential for radon risk and counties in Zone 3 have a predicted average radon screening level less than 2 pCi/L. Zone 2 has a moderate potential for radon risk and counties in Zone 2 have a predicted average radon screening level between 2 and 4 pCi/L. Zone 1 has the highest potential risk for elevated levels of radon. Counties in Zone 1 have a predicted average radon screening level greater than 4 pCi/L.

If the reading is 2 pCi/L or higher than the home needs to have Radon mitigation performed to prevent exposure to elevated levels of radon gas. The EPA radon gas ratings for Delaware are as follows;

New Castle County – Zone 2 (Moderate Potential)

Kent County –   Zone 1 (Low Potential)

Sussex County –   Zone 1 (Low Potential)

Lead Inspection

Homes built prior to 1978 may contain lead based paint and other products with lead. Lead was found to be a hazardous substance and has been outlawed in the use of paint.

If you are buying any property that was build before 1978, you should get a Lead Visual Inspection from a Delaware State Certified Lead Inspector as your first step.

Lead Facts

- Lead paint was banned in U.S. residential paint in 1978

- Children under six are most at risk

- Lead poisoning causes learning and developmental disabilities

- The primary cause is tiny particles of lead dust from deteriorated paint or from painted surfaces disturbed during remodeling, repair or renovation.

- Lead dust is so tiny in fact it passes through most mask and filters.

- Lead poisoning affects adults as well as kids.

The Addendum for Repairs

Once complete your inspections, your real estate agent will use the findings in each report to generate a list of items that you are going to ask the seller to repair or replace. The items are listed on an addendum to the sales contract that the real agent will write up. The seller can respond to your addendum in three ways; accept it as is, counter offer, or refuse it. The seller is under no obligation to fix anything in the home. If you want something fixed and the seller refuses to fix it then the sales contract is terminated and you will receive your deposit money back. You will not be reimbursed for the cost of your inspections or the appraisal.

The seller has a certain number of days to respond to the addendum. It is spelled out in the sales contract exactly how long they have to respond. Once the terms of the addendum are worked out, both parties sign it and it is now an official part of the sales contract. The agreed upon repairs must be completed before settlement.

The Title Search, Report, Abstract, & Insurance

A **title report** shows the current condition of the title, including current liens and easements and other encumbrances. A **title insurance policy** insures the accuracy of the title report. An **abstract of title** is a brief history of the title, but does not provide any insurance against claims to the title like title insurance does.

Your real estate settlement attorney will order a title search to be performed on the property that you are buying. The search will see if there are any judgments or liens that have been placed against the property. The search will confirm that the seller is the owner of record and that no other interested parties have claim to the title. It will make sure there are no unsatisfied liens against the property; such as any old mortgages that were not properly cleared. The attorney will also perform a search on the buyers and the sellers to make sure there are no judgments or liens that would prevent the transaction from taking place. Your lender will not let you take title with any unpaid liens or judgments against you because they could be attached to the house once you buy it.

Once the title search is returned to the attorney, the attorney will provide the lender with a title report and title abstract all together in what is called the title binder.

Once the title search is done and settlement is complete, the title company will issue a title insurance policy insuring the title. The insurance policy insures against any liens or claims against the home that might have been missed in the original title search. You typically buy two policies, one for the lender (Lender Policy) and one for yourself (Owners Policy). The lender requires you to buy their policy; you are not required to buy your own policy. The title insurance protects you in case there is a claim against the title. You should always buy your own title insurance policy to protect yourself.

Title Insurance Overview

Basic Owner's Title Policy Coverage:

1. Clear Title to the property
2. Incorrect signatures on documents
3. Forgery, fraud
4. Defective recordation
5. Restrictive covenants
6. Encumbrances or judgments

Basic Lender's Title Policy Coverage:

1. Mechanic's liens and unrecorded liens
2. Unrecorded easements and access rights
3. Defects and other unrecorded documents

Extended Owner's Coverage

1. Building permit violations from previous owners
2. Subdivision maps
3. Covenant violations from previous owners
4. Living trusts
5. Structure damage from mineral extractions
6. Variety of encroachments and forgeries after title insurance is issued

You only pay the title insurance premium once for your Owner's Policy and it protects you for as long as you own the home.

You will also need to decide how you will take title to the property. Title to real property in Delaware may be held by individuals, either in sole ownership or co-ownership. Co-ownership of property occurs when two or more people hold title to a property.

Sole Ownership Options for Delaware

Single man or single woman – a man or woman who has never been married

Unmarried man or woman – a man or woman who has been legally married but is now legally divorced.

Married Man or Married woman – a man or woman who is married but their spouse is not going on the title.

Co-Ownership Options for Delaware

Delaware recognizes the following types of co-ownership: **tenancy in common** and **joint tenancy**, but not tenancy by entirety and community property. A grant of ownership of real estate to two or more persons is presumed to create a tenancy in common, unless a joint tenancy is specifically created. Delaware Code §25-311, 701

The Survey

A property survey is ordered by the real estate attorney and it is performed by a surveyor. The mortgage company and the title insurance company typically require that the survey be done. The survey must be recent, done within the last 6 months of the closing date. A surveyor draws a map that shows the property boundaries as well as where the house, garage, and other features, such as boundary fences or walls, driveways and barns and sheds, are located. It also reveals easements such as power poles, sewer manholes, catch basins, drainage ditches, telephone and cable TV boxes. This information is especially important when the homeowner or a neighbor undertakes to build improvements.

The survey will also reveal if there were any structures or additions built without the proper permit from the County. The survey will ensure property meets the county building code in regards to the structures proximity to the boundaries. You will receive a copy of the survey at settlement and the attorney should review it with you at that time. It is important that you keep the survey somewhere safe like a fireproof lockbox because the county will require it if you ever choose to make any improvements to the property.

Hazard Insurance (Homeowners Insurance)

Your lender will require that you have homeowners insurance on the property that is effective the date of settlement. The lender calls the insurance Hazard Insurance, but everybody else calls it homeowners insurance. Homeowners insurance is designed to repair or replace your home in the event it is damaged or destroyed. Homeowners insurance also protects the valuables within the residence in the event they are stolen or destroyed; this is termed personal property coverage on the policy. Your homeowners insurance also provides you with personal liability insurance. This protects you in case you are named as a defendant in a civil lawsuit. It will not cover the cost of a criminal trial or any penalty set forth in a criminal trial.

Your lender requires you to have homeowners insurance so that they are protected in the event of a disaster. Since your home is the collateral used to secure your mortgage, the lender wants to make sure there is adequate protection in case the home was to have a disaster. The lender is going to require that you have coverage in the amount at least equal to the loan amount so that their money is protected.

Types of Coverage

Dwelling Insurance: pays for damages to the structure of the home, outbuildings, detached garages, etc.

Personal Property: covers household items, including furniture, clothing, appliances and electronics which are damaged or stolen.

Liability Insurance: protects you against financial loss if you are found legally responsible for someone else's injury or property damage.

Medical Payments: pays the medical bills for anyone injured on your property

Loss of Use: covers living expenses if your property is destroyed or too damaged to live in while being repaired.

Flood Insurance

Flooding can happen anywhere, but certain areas are especially prone to serious flooding. To help communities understand their risk, flood maps (Flood Insurance Rate Maps, FIRMs) have been created to show the locations of high-risk, moderate-to-low risk, and undetermined-risk areas. Here are the definitions for each:

High-risk areas (Special Flood Hazard Area or SFHA)
High-risk areas have at least a 1% annual chance of flooding, which equates to a 26% chance of flooding over the life of a 30-year mortgage. All homeowners in these areas with mortgages from federally regulated or insured lenders are required to buy flood insurance. They are shown on the flood maps as zones labeled with the letters A or V.

Moderate-to-low risk areas (Non-Special Flood Hazard Area or NSFHA)
In moderate-to-low risk areas, the risk of being flooded is reduced, but not completely removed. These areas are outside the 1% annual flood-risk floodplain areas, so flood insurance isn't required, but it is recommended for all property owners and renters. They are shown on flood maps as zones labeled with the letters B, C or X (or a shaded X).

Undetermined-risk areas
No flood-hazard analysis has been conducted in these areas, but a flood risk still exists. Flood insurance rates reflect the uncertainty of the flood risk. These areas are labeled with the letter D on the flood maps.

Your lender will order a Flood Certificate to determine if your property is in a flood plain. If the property you are buying is determined to be located in a High Risk Area then you are required to purchase flood insurance. Flood insurance is purchased separate from your Homeowners Insurance.

The Underwriting Process

Once you have completed your official mortgage application your loan will move to processing. The loan processor will complete all of the following tasks in order to prepare your loan to be submitted to underwriting;

1) Order Appraisal, Title Search, & Survey

2) Verify income & employment information for past 2 years

3) Verify Residence & rental history for past 2 years

4) Verify assets and gift funds

5) Verify Homeowners insurance information & proper coverage

6) Order past two year tax transcripts from the IRS

7) Receive appraisal and review for repairs & check value

8) Request any missing documentation from borrower

9) Receive and Review any required inspections

10) Order Flood Certificate

11) Receive and review Title Report & Survey

Once this has all been completed the file is ready to be submitted to underwriting. The underwriter will review all the documentation in the file and make sure everything meets the loan guidelines for the loan program that is being used.

The underwriter will issue one of the following decisions after reviewing the file:

Approved with conditions

Suspended

Denied

Counteroffer

Approved with conditions – This is the decision you want from the underwriter. It means you have met all the guidelines for the loan program but still need several items in order to clear the loan for closing. Your mortgage planner will issue a Mortgage Commitment Letter to the real estate agents and the seller. This lets everybody know that you are conditionally approved for the loan and will state what items are needed in order to clear the loan for closing.

Suspended - This decision means that you didn't provide enough information for the loan to meet all the guidelines. The reason for the suspense will be identified. If you can provide the missing information then your loan will be approved with conditions and your mortgage commitment letter will be issued. If you cannot satisfy the suspense condition then your loan will be denied.

Denied – A loan denial means you were not approved for the loan by the underwriter because your file didn't meet the loan guidelines. The specific reason for the denial will be given. You can appeal the denial if you feel that you can provide sufficient proof that overcomes the reason for the denial.

Counter Offer – The underwriter may make a counteroffer in order to approve your loan. This could be asking for more of a down payment in order to qualify. For example if you are getting an FHA loan with a minimum of 3.5% down payment, the underwriter may counter with a 5% or 10% down payment in order to approve the loan. If you accept the counter offer then the loan will move to approved with conditions. If you don't accept the counter offer then the loan moves to denied.

Clear to Close

Once you get an approval, you will need to provide all of the items listed by your mortgage planner as conditions that are needed to clear the loan to close. Once all the conditions have been received, the processor will submit the loan back to the underwriter to have the conditions cleared. The underwriter will review the conditions and if acceptable, you will receive the Clear to Close.

Your loan file will then be sent to the closing department. The closing department will review your file by performing an audit. The audit will verify all the documentation matches. For example, making sure the borrower's names are all correct on the appraisal, title paperwork, and loan paperwork. Audit will verify the homeowners insurance is adequate. Most importantly the audit will verify that the APR hasn't changed by more than a 1/8 of a percentage from what was last disclosed to you. If it has changed by more than a 1/8 of a percentage then the truth in lending and the good faith estimate must be re-disclosed to you and you must wait at least 3 business days before you can settle if done in person. If mailed to you, then you must wait 6 business days before you can close the loan. This is a federal law that went into effect on August 1, 2009.

Once the audit is complete you loan is assigned to a closer who will draw up all the documents that you will be signing at the settlement. The closing instructions and loan documents are typically e-mailed to the closing agent which is your real estate attorney or his paralegal. The closing agent will draw up your Final HUD settlement sheet. This will show you all your closing figures and the seller's closing figures on the same document. This will have your final figure for how much money you need to bring to the settlement. You will need to get a cashier's check or a certified check made payable to the real estate attorney.

The lender will wire the money into the attorney's account. The attorney collects all the money and then will distribute it after the settlement to whoever is supposed to receive it.

The Final Walk Thru

Your real estate agent will schedule a final walk thru 24-48 hours before the scheduled settlement. It is very important that you have your final walk thru. This is where you and your agent check to make sure the property is in the same condition as when you agreed to buy it. You will also verify that any repairs that were agreed upon have been completed. You and your agent will also verify that any property that was supposed to be included in the sale has been left, such as stove, refrigerator, window treatments, etc. You also want to verify that the seller has removed all of their items from the house and that no trash has been left behind.

If any issues come up on the final walk thru, your agent and your attorney will handle getting it resolved with the seller.

Final Walk Thru Checklist

- Repairs you have requested have been completed. Obtain copies of paid bills & warranties.
- No Major Changes to the property since last viewed it.
- Al items that were included are still there – draperies, lighting fixtures, etc
- Screens & Storm windows are in place or stored.
- All appliances are operating, such as the dishwasher, washer, dryer, oven, etc.
- Doorbell and alarm are operational.
- Hot water heater is working.
- No plants or shrubs have been removed from the yard.
- Heating and air conditioning system is working.
- Garage door opener and other remotes are available.
- Instruction books and warranties on appliances and fixtures are available.
- All personal items of the sellers and all debris have been removed. Check the basement, attic, and every room, closet, and crawlspace.

The Closing or Settlement

This is the last step in the purchase process. You will meet the seller at the attorney's office to sign all of the paperwork to transfer the deed of the property from the seller to you. You will sign all of the loan paperwork as well which is your mortgage. You receive the keys to the house and when you leave the attorney's office, you own the house!!

Home Warranty

A home warranty is a service contract that covers the repair or replacement of many of the most frequently occurring breakdowns of home system components and appliances for the first year you own the home. Everything is not covered by the warranty; however most of the system components and appliances that breakdown frequently are covered.

Your home is most likely one of your biggest investments. Unexpected repair or replacement costs can easily strain your budget. With the home warranty, any time you have a problem with one of the covered systems, you call the warranty company and they will send out a certified technician to diagnose and fix the problem. All you pay is a low service fee depending on which company you choose and which plan you bought. You can use the plan as many times as you wish during the contract period.

Most basic home warranties cover the following systems:

Heating System	Plumbing System	Electrical System
Water Heater	Ceiling Fans	Garbage Disposal
Dishwasher	Built-in Microwave	Ductwork
Exhaust Fan	Plumbing Stoppages	
Oven/Range/Cooktops		

You can pay more to expand your coverage to these systems:

Central A/C	Refrigerator	Clothes Washer
Clothes Dryer	Garage Door Opener	Well Pump
Pool	Spa	

All Home Warranty companies require you to use their service reps to come out and diagnose and fix problems. If you call a contractor yourself to fix a problem, it will not be covered by the Home Warranty Company.

Dos & Don'ts During the Loan Process

1) Do not change jobs, become self-employed or quit your job,
2) Do not buy a car, truck or van
3) Do not use charge cards excessively or let accounts fall behind in payments
4) Do not spend money you have set aside for closing.
5) Do not omit debts or liabilities from your loan application.
6) Do not buy furniture or appliances on credit.
7) Do not originate any inquiries into your credit.
8) Do not make any deposits into your bank account that cannot be sourced.
9) Do not change bank accounts.
10) Do not co-sign a loan for anyone.
11) Do call your mortgage planner if you have any questions.
12) Do not fall behind on your rent.
13) Do continue to pay all your bills on time.
14) Do Not Deposit any Cash into your bank account that cannot be sourced.

Chapter 10

What Happens After the Loan Closes?

You went to the attorney's office and completed the transaction and you now have the keys to your new home, what do you do and what happens next?

Post Closing Checklist:

1) Transfer all utilities to your name (Appendix D)

2) Change all the locks on your new home

3) Be sure you completed change of address and mail forwarding with the post office

4) Move all your stuff into your new home

5) Complete homeowner's insurance inventory of all personal property. Put list with copy of policy in another location such as safety deposit box or relatives house in case of fire.

6) Put Deed, Survey, mortgage note, and title insurance policy into fire proof lockbox.

7) Make your first mortgage payment.

It is very important that you put the date of your first mortgage payment on your calendar. You will receive a *First Payment Coupon* at settlement as part of your settlement documents. Keep this payment coupon in a safe place as you may not receive your mortgage payment coupon booklet or statement before your first mortgage payment is due. If this happens you are still responsible for making the mortgage payment on time that is why you are provided with a first payment coupon at settlement.

Loan Servicing

I common question that comes up from new home owners is, "Who do I make my mortgage payments to?" The person that you write your mortgage check to is called the "loan servicer". If you worked with a mortgage broker to obtain your mortgage, you will not make your mortgage payments to the broker. You will make your mortgage payments to the lender that the broker placed your loan with.

If you worked with a mortgage banker to obtain your mortgage then that bank is your lender and will be your loan servicer so you will write your check to the mortgage bank every month.

Your loan can also be sold from one mortgage lender to another mortgage lender this is called transferring of servicing.. This would change who your loan servicer is but cannot change the rate or the terms of the loan. Sometimes banks will sell your loan before your loan even closes. This is very common and if this happens to you, it will be disclosed to you at settlement that your loan has been sold.

It is very common for mortgage loans to be sold from one bank to another so don't be concerned or alarmed if you loan is sold. It can happen right away or 2, 5 or even 10 years into your loan.

The Escrow Account

Your lender will setup an escrow account for you to pay your yearly real estate property taxes and your yearly homeowner's insurance premium if they are included in your monthly mortgage payment.

The escrow account must be handled according to Section 10 of the RESPA law. It states borrower must receive an initial escrow account statement at settlement and one annually thereafter. The law also limits the amount the lender can require to be held in the escrow account; the maximum is the amounts needed to pay all items in escrow plus a 2 month cushion. The yearend annual statement must be provided to the borrower within 30 days after computation is done by the lender.

If your escrow account has a shortage which means either your taxes or your homeowner's insurance or both increased this caused the lender to have to make up the difference. You will get an escrow account shortage notice along with your annual statement. The lender will give you the option of paying the shortage within 30 days or the option to break it up over 12 payments and have it added to your monthly mortgage payment. If you choose the second option, your monthly mortgage payment will increase.

Chapter 11

Delaware Down-Payment Assistant Programs

Delaware Revenue Bond Program

Delaware First Time Home Buyers have several options for first time home buyer programs. The State of Delaware has several programs available for home buyers in all 3 counties (New Castle, Kent, and Sussex) of Delaware. The program is governed by The Delaware State Housing Authority. The program is called The **Single Family Mortgage Revenue Bond Program**. The program is commonly referred to as the Delaware First Time Home Buyer Program but is only one of many different programs available in Delaware.

This statewide program provides first mortgage financing at below-market interest rates to low- and moderate-income Delaware homebuyers who have not owned a home in the past three years. The state does not make these loans; you must contact one of the participating lenders. If you would like to apply or get more information please call me at 302-703-0727 or send an e-mail to DelawareMortgages@yahoo.com

The program has income limitations for people to be eligible for the program. The income limits are based on the number of people in the household and the county where the property is located.

There are also restrictions on the maximum purchase price of the property. For New Castle County the maximum purchase price is $366,920 for a 1 unit property. Kent County has a maximum purchase price of $328,762 for a 1 unit property. Sussex County has a maximum $327,670 for a 1 unit property.

The interest rate on the loan is set by the state of Delaware and is the same no matter which lender you use to get the loan. The lender must be on the approved list. The current interest rate changes each time the state of Delaware issues a new bond.

You are required to complete a home buyer counseling program provide by one of the approved housing agencies in Delaware in order to be eligible for the program. You also must be aware that if you may have to pay a recapture tax to the IRS if you sell the house in the first 9 years. If your household income goes above the income limits for the program before you sell in the first 9 years then you will be assessed a recapture tax from the IRS. So if you are planning on selling the house in the first 9 years then you may want to consider if you want to use this program.

Delaware Second Mortgage Assistance Loan (SMAL)

The loan provides down-payment and closing cost assistance up to $10,000. The funds can run out so you must check that they are available. The loan can only be used in conjunction with the Delaware Single Mortgage Revenue Bond Program Loan.

You must use a participating lender in that is approved by DSHA. Here is link for an approved lender www.PRMIDelaware.com. The borrower must also complete a U.S. Department of Housing and Urban Development (HUD) approved housing counseling program. Most programs in Delaware charge a $100 fee and it is typically 8 hours of counseling.

There are income restrictions for the program so must be under the income limit and there are also loan limits for the purchase which are county specific. All properties using the SMAL loan must be inspected by an ASHI or NACHI home inspector. The $10,000 is a LOAN and is recorded as second mortgage against the property. There is a 6% interest that is charged every year on the loan. The loan is deferred for 30 years but incurs interest the whole time. The loan must also be paid in full if you sell the house, refinance the house, or no longer use the home as your primary residence.

The SMAL loan is a good option for someone who has no other access to money for down payment, but if you qualify for another program or have a 401k, then this is probably not the best option because of the 6% interest that is charged each year on the outstanding principle balance.

New Castle County Down Payment Assistance Programs

New Castle County has three First Time Home Buyer Programs; Down Payment Settlement Program (DPS), the Home Owner Incentive Program (HIP), and the Home Town Heroes First Time Home Buyer Program.

The **New Castle County Down Payment Settlement Program** gives first time home buyers deferred payment loans for up to $5,000 to cover customary settlement costs and up to half of the required down payment to purchase a home located in New Castle County, Delaware. The loan is an 8 year loan that requires no payment for the first 3 years of the loan. The loan is then repaid over the last 5 years at a rate of 3%. If loan is paid off in first 3 years then no interest is charged. The residence must be borrower's primary residence throughout the duration of the loan.

You can use this loan program for existing residential properties or new construction located in New Castle County. The maximum selling price of the home is the FHA 203b program county limit of $420,000 for 2009. The Property must be inspected by an ASHI or NAHI certified home inspector as a condition of sale. Certain DPS funding may require property to pass RIB (Residential International Building) Code and NCC adopted codes. All homes built prior to 1978 must meet HUD requirements regarding lead paint. This means you need a visual lead inspection from a lead inspector that is HUD & Delaware certified.

The Minimum loan amount is $1,000 and the maximum loan amount is $5,000. The loan must be paid in full upon the sale of your property or the transfer of ownership. If you refinance you will also need to pay the loan off because it is recorded as a second mortgage and New Castle County will not re-subordinate the loan to second position when you pay off the first mortgage to refinance into a new first mortgage. You must have a minimum cash contribution of $500.

The **New Castle County Home Owner Incentive Program (HIP)** is a deferred loan program to help home buyers purchase homes in targeted neighborhoods. The program will give a loan for up to 6% of the sales price for a maximum of $10,000. The interest rate is 0% and no payments are required. The loan must be paid in full when home is sold or if no longer primary residence. The program is only available in identified targeted neighborhoods. The maximum sale price is $178,100. You do not have to be a first time home buyer to qualify for this program.

The property must be inspected by ASHI or NAHI certified home inspector as a condition of the sale. All homes built prior to 1978 must have a lead paint visual inspection. To obtain a list of the targeted neighborhoods that qualify for this program feel free to contact me at 302-703-0727 or send an e-mail to DelawareMortgages@yahoo.com.

Both of these assistance programs require you to take 8 hours of home buyer's education from approved home buying counselor. Both of these programs have income restrictions.

The income guidelines for these two loans for 2011 are as follows:

1 Person Household: $43,900

2 Person Household: $50,150

3 Person Household: $56,400

4 Person Household: $62,650

5 Person Household: $67,780

6 Person Household: $72,700

7 Person Household: $77,700

8 Person Household: $82,700

The New Castle County ADDI Program

The NCC American Dream Down Payment Initiative (ADDI) is a down payment assistance program that created as part of the NSP funds distributed to the State of Delaware. The program provides a loan for down payment assistance for up to 6% of the purchase price with a maximum of $10,000. The interest rate is 0% and the loan is deferred for 5 years with no payments. After 5 years the loan is forgiven and never has to be paid off as long as the borrower has remained the owner occupant of the property.

You must be a First Time Home Buyer to qualify and you must attend 8 hours of home counseling. The maximum purchase price is $202,900 and you must be under the income limitation of the program. You are required to get a home inspection and visual lead inspection if the house is built before 1978.

You can only use the program to purchase NSP homes located in New Castle County, Delaware.

Eligible Income Limitations for ADDI Program is 80% of median income for 2011 it is as follows:

Household size	Maximum Income
1 Person	$43,900
2 Person	$50,150
3 Person	$56,400
4 Person	$62,650
5 Person	$67,700
6 Person	$72,700
7 Person	$77,700
8 Person	$82,700

PROS:

- No Payments for 5 years and then Forgive!
- Can use any first mortgage program or approved lender
- Not counted in DTI calculation

CONS:

- Can only use on NSP homes in New Castle County
- Income Restrictions
- Must live in house as primary residence for 5 years
- Required to have home inspection and lead inspection

The New Castle County NSP Program

The NCC NSP program is a down payment assistance program that is similar to the ADDI program but is limited to just 3% of the purchase price with a maximum of $10,000. The interest rate is 0% and the loan is deferred for 5 years with no payments. After 5 years the loan is forgiven and never has to be paid off as long as the borrower has remained the owner occupant of the property.

You must be a First Time Home Buyer to qualify and you must attend 8 hours of home counseling. The maximum purchase price is $202,900 and you must be under the income limitation of the program. You are required to get a home inspection and visual lead inspection if the house is built before 1978.

You can only use the program to purchase NSP homes located in New Castle County, Delaware. The program is for people who wish to buy one of these homes but are above the 80% median income but below 120% of the median income.

City of Newark Home Owner Assistance Programs

The city of Newark, Delaware has three programs that can benefit first time home buyers; Promoting Owner Occupancy of Homes (POOH), Home Buyer's Incentive Program, and the Home Buyer's Assistance Program.

The **POOH** program promotes and encourages the owner occupancy of homes in Newark by providing interest free, deferred payment loans of up to $50,000 towards the purchase of any single-family home in the City with a valid rental permit. Rental Permits for homes to be purchased must have been issued a minimum of two years from the date of application. The loan will be secured by a second mortgage against the property. Loan repayment will be required at the time of sale or transfer of the property, and will include the full principle amount plus a percentage of the increased value of the home during the borrower's ownership in direct proportion to the amount loaned by the City of Newark at the time of settlement. For example, if the total value of the City POOH loan consisted of 20% of the original purchase price, then the City would receive as loan repayment 20% of the net appreciation, plus the principle amount.

The **Home Buyer Incentive Program** provides funds to income-qualified first time homebuyers to purchase affordable housing. The program provides interest free deferred loans up to $5,000 to be used for settlement/closing costs and up to 50% of down payment for homes purchased within the City of Newark. The loans will be secured by a second mortgage on the home to be purchased. The full balance of the loan becomes payable upon title transfer of the residence or if the homeowner converts the property into a rental.

The **Home Buyer Assistance Program** provides low interest monthly pay back loans up to $15,000 at one percent (1%) below the Federal Home Loan Market Interest Rate. The loans will be secured by a second mortgage on the home to be purchased. To qualify, homebuyers must be willing to buy a home within target areas of the City of Newark and remain the owner occupants in the house for at least six years.

City of Wilmington HAP Program

The City of Wilmington has a Homebuyer Assistance Program (HAP) that provides a deferred loan for up to $10,000 to qualified homebuyers to purchase homes in the City of Wilmington within the 19801, 19802, and 19805 zip codes.

Eligible properties are homes that are within the target zip codes that have been vacant for a period of at least 90 days and have not been redeveloped with NSP funds. Applicants do not have to be first time home buyers but are required to complete 8 hours of home buyer counseling.

Borrowers are free to use any first mortgage program but must get a fixed rate mortgage. The household income must be equal to or below the limits for the program. The purchase price cannot exceed HUD limits. The property must be purchases at a 1% discount based upon appraised value.

Applicants must apply by June 30, 2011 and settle by August 30, 2011. Borrower must have ratified sales contract in order to apply.

Eligible Income Limitations for HAP Program

Household size	Maximum Income
1 Person	$65,750
2 Person	$75,150
3 Person	$84,550
4 Person	$93,950
5 Person	$101,500
6 Person	$109,000

Delawareans Save! IDA Program

The Delawareans Save! Individual Development Account Program (IDA) is a special savings program that assists people in saving for the purchase of a home. It will match the savings for the purpose of buying a home.

You must attend information session and eligibility appointment offered by IDA partner site. You must open an IDA savings account at either Artisans Bank or Wilmington Trust Company.

You must save a minimum of $25 a month up to a maximum of $250 per month for a minimum of 6 months and a maximum of 36 months. The maximum that you may save and get match is $1,500 per person or $3,000 per household. If you save $1,500 IDA matches it with $2,250 for a total of $3,750.

After completing the qualifications of the program you meet with counselor and complete the withdrawal request and a check will be issued to help with the purchase of the new home.

Eligible Income Limitations for IDA Program

Household size	Maximum Income
1 Person	$21,780
2 Person (2 adults)	$29,420
2 Person (1 Adult/1child)	$36,052
3 Person	$37,060
4 Person	$44,964
5 Person	$52,340
6 Person	$59,980
7 Person	$67,620
8 Person	$75,260

You must be a resident of Delaware to participate. Your total assets must be less than $10,000 NOT including a primary residence and a car.

For more information on any of the Delaware Down Payment Assistance Programs, please visit www.DelawareFirstTimeHomeBuyerBook.com/DPA.

Chapter 12

Protecting Your Investment & Your Family

Once you have bought your home you must take the steps to protect your investment and your family. You need to take the following steps in order to protect yourself;

Step 1 – Have a Last Will & Testament Written

Step 2 – Get the proper life insurance to protect your family

Step 3 – Get the proper disability insurance

Step 4 – Look into umbrella policy for home & auto insurance

You need a Will to make sure your assets are passed on as you want them to be and to avoid your heirs having to be tied up in probate court. You can write a will yourself with software programs and have it notarized or you can have an attorney prepare a will for you.

You will need enough life insurance to cover the replacement of your income so that your family can still pay all the bills now and into the future. Life insurance should be viewed as income protection. You have the option of getting a term policy or permanent insurance.

Disability insurance is the most overlooked insurance, but it is the one most people need above all others. 1 in 8 people are likely to suffer a disability before the age of 65 that lasts 90 days or more. 48% of all mortgage foreclosures are caused by a disability occurring.

We live in a society that is compelled to sue anybody at the drop of a hat. As soon as you start to accumulate wealth there will be somebody waiting to try and sue you to take it. An umbrella policy is a personal liability policy that protects you for both your home and auto in case you case an injury to someone and they sue you personally. You need to have home and auto insurance with same carrier in order to get an umbrella policy. Typically you get a $1,000,000 personal liability rider to the policy.

You need to look into the following areas to protect your family:

1. Providing educational funds for children.
2. Retirement planning.
3. Providing funds for long-term nursing home care in the future.
4. Involvement in financial planning by the spouse.
5. Saving a fixed percentage of income.
6. A review of existing property insurance.
7. Insurance of spouse and children.
8. Assuring an income during periods of disability.
9. In the event of death, paying off the mortgage and other debts.
10. In the event of death, allowing the family members to retain their existing lifestyle.

About The Author

John R. Thomas was born in Wilmington Delaware. He graduated from Glasgow High School in Newark, Delaware with the class of 1990. John went on to earn a Bachelors Degree of Physics Education from the University of Delaware. He went on to earn his Master Degree in Curriculum & Instruction from Delaware State University.

John is happily married to his beautiful wife Bernadette and they have two wonderful children Maddie and Max. They live in Newark, Delaware. John taught physics and physical science at Delcastle High School for over 10 years. He owned a local franchise of SERVPRO, a National Cleaning and Restoration Company. John was a national kickboxing champion and state boxing champion. He currently referees boxing, kickboxing, and mixed martial arts matches as well as help train fighters at Jack's Gym in Newark, Delaware.

John has been helping people obtain financing for over 10 years. He is currently the branch manager for a National Mortgage Banker. He specializes in First Time Home Buyers and presents monthly seminars to help educate buyers about the home buying process. He has been a featured guest on local TV show (The Congo Hour) to discuss mortgages and home ownership. John enjoys helping people buy homes and manage their current mortgages to help them produce long term wealth.

John is truly passionate about his profession, and the result is that nearly 100% of his business is by referral from satisfied clients, trusted financial advisors and the most experienced realtors in Delaware. John's mission is to carefully guide clients through the entire home loan process, so that they feel confident as they make choices about the many options available for their financing strategy. With many years and a wide range of experience in the mortgage industry, John's dedicated team stands ready to assist each and every step of the way.

Please feel free to visit John's Website at www.DelawareMortgageLoans.net for more information.

You can also contact John by writing to the following address or calling him at the office.

John R. Thomas

248 E Chestnut Hill Rd

Newark, DE 19713

302-703-0727 Office

DelawareMortgages@yahoo.com

Appendix A:

Understanding ARMs

Adjustable Rate Mortgages (ARMs) are loans with interest rates that change. ARMs usually start with lower monthly payments than fixed rate mortgages. With a fixed rate mortgage, the interest rate stays the same during the life of the loan. With an ARM, the interest rate changes periodically, usually in relation to an index, and payments may go up or down accordingly.

Lenders generally charge lower interests rates on ARMs than on fixed rate mortgages. This could potentially save you a lot of money because you will be paying less interest. When considering whether an ARM makes sense or not, you must first consider how long you will keep the loan you are getting. If you will probably refinance or sell the home in the next 3-5 years than you might want to consider a 5-year ARM. This would have the interest rate fixed for the first 5 years of the loan and then it could adjust either up or down. The 5-year ARM typically has a lower interest rate than a 30 year fixed rate mortgage by about 0.25% lower so you could potentially save a lot of money.

When you get an ARM you must consider what your rate could adjust to after the initial fixed period has expired. For example on the 5-year ARM, your rate is fixed for the first five years of the loan and then will adjust. You must understand how to calculate how high your interest rate can adjust. Your lender should explain how often your rate will adjust and by how much it will adjust so that you can plan accordingly. The lender should explain what the lifetime cap is on the loan, which is the highest the interest could adjust for the life of the loan. For example if the loan has a cap of 9.9% then the most your interest could increased to is 9.9% and can never go higher.

The important factors with an ARM are Initial Rate, Fully Indexed Rate, Margin, Index, & Cap. You will be given an initial rate on an ARM and an initial term. After the term your rate will adjust based on the adjustment period, the margin, and the index. The interest rate that you pay after the initial fixed period is called the Fully Indexed Rate. This is calculated by taking the index and adding the margin to it.

Example:

Index – 3.55%

Margin – 3.0%

Fully Indexed Rate – 6.55%

The margin is fixed and is set by the lender when you obtain the loan. The way the ARM adjusts is the index will go up and down depending on the market and the economy. So if the index were to go down by 1.0% in our example above the Fully Indexed Rate would drop to 5.55%. If the index were to go up instead by 1.0% then your rate would increase to 7.55%.

The most commonly used indexes are:
• The **London Interbank Offered Rate Index** (LIBOR). This is an average of the interest rates that major international banks charge each other to borrow U.S. dollars in the London money market. It is published daily by the British Bankers' Association. LIBOR tends to move and adjust rapidly to changes in interest rates (i.e., most preferred when rates may be falling).
• A monthly **Cost-of-Funds Index** (COFI). COFI is the acronym for the 11th District Monthly Weighted Average Cost of Funds Index. This is a rate that reflects the interest expenses on savings deposits reported for a given month by Arizona, California, and Nevada savings institutions that are members of the Federal Home Loan Bank of San Francisco. Since the interest on many types of deposits may remain fixed for a period, COFI does not change as rapidly as other indexes and is most preferred when rates may be rising.

• The **One-Year Constant Maturity Treasury Rate** (CMT). This is an average yield on United States Treasury securities adjusted to a constant maturity of one year, as made available by the Federal Reserve Board.

The initial rate and payment amount on an ARM will remain in effect for a limited period of time - ranging from just 1 month to 5 years or more. For some ARMs, the initial rate and payment can vary greatly from the rates and payments later in the loan term. Even if interest rates are stable, your rates and payments could change a lot. If lenders or brokers quote the initial rate and payment on a loan, ask them for the annual percentage rate (APR). If the APR is significantly higher than the initial rate, then it is likely that your rate and payments will be a lot higher when the loan adjusts, even if general interest rates remain the same.

With most ARMs, the interest rate and monthly payment change every month, quarter, year, 3 years, or 5 years. The period between rate changes is called the adjustment period. For example, a loan with an adjustment period of 1 year is called a 1-year ARM, and the interest rate and payment can change once every year; a loan with a 3 year adjustment period is called a 3-year ARM.

Your ARM loan will also have either a payment cap or a periodic adjustment cap. A payment cap is a cap on the amount the payment can increase at each adjustment. If the payment cap keeps the payment below what is necessary to pay the interest, then the interest will be added to the principal balance.

A periodic adjustment cap is a cap on how much the interest rate can change either up or down on any one adjustment. For example if the index rose 3% but the loan has a 2% periodic adjustment cap, then the rate can only rise by 2%.

Lenders must give you written information on each type of ARM loan you are interested in. The information must include the terms and conditions for each loan, including information about the index and margin, how your rate will be calculated, how often your rate can change, limits on changes (or caps), an example of how high your monthly payment might go, and other ARM features such as negative amortization.

Appendix B:

What is all the hype with Foreclosures?

First Time Home Buyers who want to get a good deal usually think about purchasing a foreclosure. A foreclosure is the process by which a bank takes ownership of a property because a home owner stops paying the mortgage. Home owners stop making payments on their mortgage for a variety of reasons which include the following;

- Laid-off, fired or quit job

- Inability to continue working due to medical conditions

- Excessive debt and mounting bill obligations

- Squabbles with co-owner, divorce

- Job transfer to another state

Before you even consider a foreclosure you need to educate yourself on what buying a foreclosure entails. There are 3 phases in a foreclosure that relate to you as the home buyer. The first phase is called pre-foreclosure, the second phase is called foreclosure, and the last phase is REO property.

Pre-foreclosure is the stage where a home owner is in default on their home mortgage and their lender has started the foreclosure process. The home owner lists their home for sale to try and sell the home before it gets foreclosed on by the bank. If the seller owes the bank more than the house is worth then the home must be listed as a short sale.

A short sale requires the lender to approve it before it can take place. For example if a house is listed for sale and the buyer and seller agree on a purchase price of $200,000 but the seller owes the bank $250,000, the bank must agree to take $50,000 less than they are owed. This process can take from four to eight months for the lender to approve the short sale so the buyer must be in a position to wait for an answer.

Just because a property is listed with short sale terms does not mean the lender will accept your offer, even if the seller accepts it. You must be prepared to wait then once the lender accepts they expect you to close in less than 30 days and will penalize you a fee per day that you go past the close date.

The second phase is the foreclosure itself. In Delaware the sheriff will auction the house off at the county court house. The bank that is foreclosing on the property usually bids first at what they are owed. If anybody else wants to bid more than the bank then they will win the auction. The bidder must put up 10% of the sale price at the auction and has about 23 days to come up with the remainder of the money. It is not possible to get a traditional mortgage to buy a foreclosure at the auction so the buyer must have access to the cash for the whole bid.

The third phase of a foreclosure is when the bank buys the property at the sheriff sale for what they are owed. The property becomes what is termed and REO which stands for Real Estate Owned. These will be listed by realtors for the banks just like any other property on the Multi List Service (MLS). These properties are bought just like any other property. You submit and offer and your realtor will negotiate with the banks realtor.

Appendix C:

Why Delaware?

Delaware is known as the First State because it was the first state in the union to ratify the U.S. Constitution. Delaware is famous for its tax free shopping; there is no sales tax in the state of Delaware.. Delaware is also known for its race track casinos and now for sports betting.

Delaware is divided into three counties shown below; 1 - **New Castle**, 2 - **Kent,** and 3 - **Sussex**. New Castle County is home to the biggest city in Delaware, which is Wilmington. Kent County is known for Dover, the Capital of Delaware. Dover is home to Dover Downs race track casino. Sussex County is known for its Delaware beaches and for its famous Outlets in Rehoboth, Delaware. Sussex County also is home to the Harrington race track casino and is the site of the Delaware State Fair.

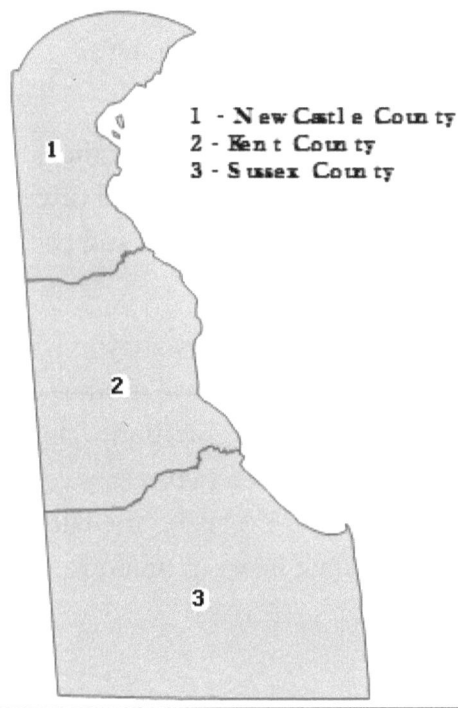

1 - New Castle County
2 - Kent County
3 - Sussex County

Brief History of Delaware:

It lies on the Atlantic Ocean and is bordered by Pennsylvania, New Jersey, and Maryland. Covering 2,026 sq mi (5,247 sq km), its capital is Dover. Originally inhabited by Algonquian tribes, Delaware's first permanent white settlement was by Swedes at Fort Christina, now Wilmington, in 1638. In 1655 New Sweden was taken by the Dutch of New Amsterdam and in 1664 by the English. Delaware was thereafter a part of New York until 1682, when it was ceded to William Penn. It was governed by Pennsylvania until 1776, although it was granted its own assembly in 1704. The first state to ratify the U.S. Constitution in 1787, it is the nation's second smallest state but one of its most densely populated.

Delaware Driver and Vehicle Information

New Residents in Delaware must obtain a driver's license within 60 days after establishing residency except for active duty military personnel. For general information on obtaining a Delaware driver's license call 302-744-2500.

You must apply in person at one of the offices of the Division of Motor Vehicles. If you have never had a valid driver license then you must pass a driver license examination and pay $12.50 fee for a five year license.

If you are becoming a new resident of Delaware you will need to register your vehicle within 60 days. You will need to get an inspection done on your car at the time of registration. The fee is $20 for a one year registration or $40 for a two year registration. Delaware also will charge a 2.75% tax on the fair market value of the car for any out of state new registration.

Appendix D:

Local Utility Information

<u>Utilities</u>

Delmarva Power (Gas & Electric)

800-375-7117

City of Newark (Gas, Electric, Water)

302-366-7085

Town of Middletown

302-378-2711

Artesian Water Co.

302-453-6930

United Water Co.

302-633-5900

Comcast (Cable/Phone/Internet)

800-226-2278

Verizon (FIOS/Phone/Internet)

800-942-5000

<u>Waste Management</u>

Delaware Sanitation

302-322-7714

Michael Leach

302-737-4090

Tri State Waste

302-622-8600

Waste Management, Inc.

800-345-7932

Appendix E:

Mortgage Laws to Protect You

1) RESPA – Real Estate Settlement Procedures Act
2) ECOA – Equal Credit Opportunity Act
3) FCRA – Fair Credit Reporting Act
4) FACTA – Fair and Accurate Credit Transactions Act
5) GLBA – Gramm-Leach-Bliley Act
6) HMDA – Home Mortgage Disclosure Act
7) CRA – Community Reinvestment Act
8) TILA – Truth in Lending Act

The Real Estate Settlement Procedures Act or RESPA was enacted in 1974 and was implemented by Regulation X. RESPA requires lenders to disclose fees and costs involved when closing home mortgages and prohibit abusive settlement practices, including payment of anything of value for a referral.

The Equal Credit Opportunity Act or ECOA was enacted in 1974 making it unlawful for creditors to discriminate in a credit transaction on the basis of sex or marital status. Regulation B was issued by the Federal Reserve Board to implement the provisions of ECOA and deals with taking, evaluating and examining applications for credit as well as how the information is collected.

ECOA prohibits lenders from discouraging applicants from applying on the basis of the following:

- Sex
- Martial Status
- Race
- Color
- Religion
- National Origin
- Age
- Receipt of Public Assistance

In order to track whether lenders are following this law, lenders are required to request the applicant's race or national origin, sex, marital status, and age. You are not required to supply this information but if you choose not to in a face to face application then the lender is required to make their best guess as to the correct information if you choose not to supply it.

ECOA also prevents lenders from discriminating based on age so not matter how old you are, you can obtain a mortgage loan. Lenders are allowed to deny credit for being too young to legally sign a contract. ECOA also requires a lender to notify a borrower within 30 days of an application of the action taken on the loan.

The Fair Credit Reporting Act or FCRA was added to the Consumer Protection Act in 1970 and its purpose to promote accuracy and fairness in the reporting of credit. FCRA allows a Credit Reporting Agency (CRA) to report negative information for up to seven years.

The Fair and Accurate Credit Transactions Act or FACTA amended the Fair Credit Reporting Act to increase the standards of credit reporting accuracy and improve the protections for consumers with regards to identity theft. FACTA requires mortgage lenders to provide the consumer with a copy of their credit scores and a notice explaining credit scores and the contact information for the credit reporting agency that provided the scores. This is typically Experian, Transunion, and Equifax.

FACTA also requires each of the three major credit reporting agencies to allow consumers to obtain a free copy of their credit report every 12 months.

The Gramm-Leach-Bliley Act or GLBA provides guidelines under which financial institutions must work in order to protect the privacy of their consumers. This Act was implemented by Regulation P and it requires financial institutions to advise the consumer of the company's information sharing practices and gives the consumer some rights as to limiting what personal information is shared.

This means that if you go to a big bank like Wells Fargo and apply for a mortgage that they have to tell you that they are going to share your information with all of their affiliates so you will be getting solicited for insurance, credit cards, car loans, checking and savings accounts, etc. The bank is also supposed to make it clear to you that you can opt out of this.

The Home Mortgage Disclosure Act or HMDA was enacted by Congress in 1974 and is implemented by Regulation C. The purpose of HMDA is to provide the public with information on how well banks are meeting the credit needs of people in the neighborhood and communities those banks serve and to help determine if there are discriminatory practices of a certain bank.

According to HMDA, each lender must report the following information for each transaction:

• The type and amount of the loan

• Whether the application was denied or resulted in the origination of the loan

• The property to which the loan relates

• The applicant's ethnicity, race, sex and annual income

The Truth in Lending Act or TILA requires the disclosure of loan terms and percentage rates in a form that supposedly makes it easier for consumers to compare loans. The TILA is implemented by Regulation Z which requires lenders to disclose something called the Annual Percentage Rate or APR. The APR is suppose to show the cost of the credit over the full term of the loan So for example you might have a note rate of 5.0% but an APR of 5.76%. The APR is not a real number in terms of anything you will pay, it is only useful as a comparison tool when comparing one lender to another if offering the same note rate. If APR is higher than that lender would have more closing costs.

Appendix F:
Pictures of Common Delaware Home Styles

The Cape Cod

The Bi-Level (Raised Ranch)

The Colonial

The Victorian

The Ranch

The Split Level

The Townhome

The Twin Home

The Condo

The Row Home

The Mobile Home

Glossary of Terms

A

Abstract of title

A historical summary provided by a title insurance company of all records affecting the title to a property.

Acceleration clause

Allows a lender to declare the entire outstanding balance of a loan immediately due and payable should a borrower violate specific loan provisions or default on the loan.

Adjustable rate mortgage (ARM)

A variable or flexible rate mortgage with an interest rate that varies according to the financial index it is based upon. To limit the borrower's risk, the ARM may have a payment or rate cap.

Amenities

Features of your home that fit your preferences and can increase the value of your property. Some examples include the number of bedrooms, bathrooms, or vicinity to public transportation.

Amortization

The liquidation of a debt by regular, usually monthly, installments of principal and interest. An amortization schedule is a table showing the payment amount, interest, principal and unpaid balance for the entire term of the loan.

Annual percentage rate (A.P.R.)

The actual interest rate, taking into account points and other finance charges, for the projected life of a mortgage. Disclosure of APR is required by the Truth-in-Lending Law and allows borrowers to compare the actual costs of different mortgage loans.

Appraisal

An estimate of a property's value as of a given date, determined by a qualified professional appraiser. The value may be based on replacement cost, the sales of comparable properties or the property's ability to produce income.

Appreciation

A property's increase in value due to inflation or economic factors.

"As is" condition

The Seller will make no repairs to the house before settlement.

Assessed Value

The valuation placed upon property by a public tax assessor for purposes of taxation.

Assessment

Charges levied against a property for tax purposes or to pay for municipality or association improvements such as curbs, sewers, or grounds maintenance.

Assignment

The transfer of a contract or a right to buy property at given rates and terms from a mortgagee to another person.

Assumption

An agreement between a buyer and a seller, requiring lender approval, where the buyer takes over the payments for a mortgage and accepts the liability. Assuming a loan can be advantageous for a buyer because there are no closing costs and the loan's interest rate may be lower than current market rates. Depending on what is in the mortgage or deed of trust, the lender may raise the interest rate, require the buyer to qualify for the mortgage, or not permit the buyer to assume the loan at all.

B

Balloon mortgage

Mortgage with a final lump sum payment that is greater than preceding payments and pays the loan in full.

Biweekly mortgage

A loan requiring payments of principal and interest at two-week intervals. This type of loan amortizes much faster than monthly payment loans. The payment for a biweekly mortgage is half what a monthly payment would be.

Bond

A certificate serving as security for payment of a debt. Bonds backed by mortgage loans are pooled together and sold in the secondary market.

Bridge loan

A loan to "bridge" the gap between the termination of one mortgage and the beginning of another, such as when a borrower purchases a new home before receiving cash proceeds from the sale of a prior home. Also known as a swing loan.

Broker

An intermediary between the borrower and the lender. The broker may represent several lending sources and charges a fee or commission for services.

Buy-down

Where the buyer pays additional discount points or makes a substantial down payment in return for a below market interest rate; or the seller offers 3-2-1 interest payment plans or pays closing costs such as the origination fee. During times of high interest rates, buy-downs may induce buyers to purchase property they may not otherwise have purchased.

C
Cap

A limit in how much an adjustable rate mortgage's monthly payment or interest rate can increase. A cap is meant to protect the borrower from large increases and may be a payment cap, an interest cap, a life-of-loan cap or an annual cap.

A **payment cap** is a limit on the monthly payment.

An **interest cap** is a limit on the amount of the interest rate.

A **life-of-loan cap** restricts the amount the interest rate can increase over the entire term of the loan.

An **annual cap** limits the amount the interest rate can increase over a twelve-month period.

Cash Reserve

A requirement of some lenders that buyers have sufficient cash remaining after closing.

Certificate of Eligibility (COE)

A certificate of eligibility is a document issued by Department of Veterans Affairs (VA) to certify a person's eligibility to obtain a VA loan.

Certificate of Occupancy (CO)

A certificate issued by the building department of the local or county government to a builder or owner, stating that the building is in proper condition to be occupied and specifying the legally permissible use.

Certificate of reasonable value (CRV)

A Veteran's Administration appraisal that establishes the maximum VA mortgage loan amount for a specified property.

Certificate of title

Document rendering an opinion on the status of a property's title based on public records.

Closed-end mortgage

A mortgage principal amount that is fixed and cannot be increased during the life of the loan.

Closing costs

Costs payable by both seller and buyer at the time of settlement, when the purchase of a property is finalized. These costs can be up to ten percent of the mortgage amount and usually include but are not limited to the following:

Cloud

A claim to the title of a property that, if valid, would prevent a purchaser from obtaining a clear title.

Collateral

Something of value pledged as security for a loan. In mortgage lending, the property itself serves as collateral for a mortgage loan. .

Commitment fee

A fee charged when an agreement is reached between a lender and a borrower for a loan at a specific rate and points and the lender guarantees to lock in that rate.

Co-mortgagor

One who is individually and jointly obligated to repay a mortgage loan and shares ownership of the property with one or more borrowers.

Condominium

An individually owned unit within a multi-unit building where others or the Condominium Owners Association share ownership of common areas such as the grounds, the parking facilities and the tennis courts.

Conforming loan

A loan that conforms to Federal National Mortgage Association (FNMA) or Federal Home Loan Mortgage Corporation (FHLMC) guidelines.

Construction loan

A short-term loan financing improvements to real estate, such as the building of a new home. The lender advances funds to the borrower as needed while construction progresses. Upon completion of the construction, the borrower must obtain permanent financing or pay the construction loan in full.

Consumer handbook on adjustable rate mortgages (C.H.A.R.M.)

A disclosure required by the federal government to be given to any borrower applying for an adjustable rate mortgage (ARM).

Conventional loan

A mortgage loan that is not insured, guaranteed or funded by the Veterans Administration (VA), the Federal Housing Administration (FHA) or Rural Economic Community Development (RECD) (formerly Farmers Home Administration).

Convertible mortgage

An adjustable rate mortgage (ARM) that allows a borrower to switch to a fixed-rate mortgage at a specified point in the loan term.

Cooperative (co-op)

A property of two or more units whose title is held by a corporation. Residents own shares in the corporation that entitle them to occupy a certain apartment or unit.

Covenants

Rules and restrictions governing the use of property.

Credit Report

An account of an individual's credit history prepared by a credit reporting agency and used by a lender in determining a loan applicant's creditworthiness.

Curtailments

The borrower's privilege to make payments on a loan's principal before they are due. Paying off a mortgage before it is due may incur a penalty if so specified in the mortgage's prepayment clause.

D

Debt

Money owed to repay someone.

Debt-to-income ratio

The ratio between a borrower's monthly payment obligations divided by his or her net effective income (FHA or VA loans) or gross monthly income (conventional loans).

Deed

The legal document conveying title to a property

Deed of trust

A document, used in many states in place of a mortgage, held by a trustee pending repayment of the loan. The advantage of a deed of trust is that the trustee does not have to go to court to proceed with foreclosure should the borrower default on the loan.

Default

Failure to make mortgage payments on a timely basis or to comply with other conditions of a mortgage.

Department of Housing and Urban Development (HUD)

The U.S. government agency that administers FHA, GNMA and other housing programs.

Depreciation

A decline in the value of a property; the opposite of "appreciation"

Discount points

Amounts paid to the lender based on the loan amount to buy the interest rate down. Each point is one percent of the loan amount; for example, two points on a $100,000 mortgage is $2,000.

Down payment

The difference between the purchase price and mortgage amount. The down payment becomes the property equity. Typically it should be cash savings, but it can also be a gift that is not to be repaid or a borrowed amount secured by assets.

Due-on-sale

A clause in a mortgage or deed of trust allowing a lender to require immediate payment of the balance of the loan if the property is sold (subject to the terms of the security instrument).

Duplex

Dwelling divided into two units.

E

Earnest money

Deposit in the form of cash or a note, given to a seller by a buyer as good faith assurance that the buyer intends to go through with the purchase of a property.

Easement

The right one party has in regard to the property of another, such as the right of a public utility company to lay lines.

Equal Credit Opportunity Act

A federal law prohibiting lenders and other creditors from discrimination based on race, color, sex, religion, national origin, age, marital status, receipt of public assistance or because an applicant has exercised his or her rights under the Consumer Credit Protection Act.

Encumbrance

A claim levied against a property, limiting the owner's ability to transfer the title. Liens and attachments are common forms of encumbrances.

Equity

The value of a property beyond any liens against it. Also referred to as owner's interest. It is the difference between what you can sell it for and what you owe the bank.

Escape clause

A provision allowing one party or more to cancel all or part of the contract if certain events fail to happen, such as the ability of the buyer to obtain financing within a specified period.

Escrow

Money placed with a third party for safekeeping either for final closing on a property or for payment of taxes and insurance throughout the year.

F

Fair market value

The price a property can realistically sell for based upon comparable selling prices of other properties in the same area.

Fannie Mae

Nickname for Federal National Mortgage Association (FNMA).

Federal Home Loan Mortgage Corporation (FHLMC or Freddie Mac)

A quasi-governmental, federally-sponsored organization that acts as a secondary market investor to buy and sell mortgage loans. FHLMC sets many of the guidelines for conventional mortgage loans, as does FNMA.

Federal Housing Administration (FHA)

An agency within the Department of Housing and Urban Development that sets standards for underwriting and insures residential mortgage loans made by private lenders. One of FHA's objectives is to ensure affordable mortgages to those with low or moderate income. FHA loans may be high loan-to-value, and they are limited by loan amount. FHA mortgage insurance requires a fee of 1.75 percent of the loan amount to be paid at closing, as well as an annual fee of 0.55 percent of the loan amount added to each monthly payment.

Federal National Mortgage Association (FNMA or Fannie Mae)

A private corporation that acts as a secondary market. investor to buy and sell mortgage loans. FNMA sets many of the guidelines for conventional mortgage loans, as does FHLMC. The major purpose of this organization is to make mortgage money more affordable and more available.

Fee simple

The maximum form of ownership, with the right to occupy a property and sell it to a buyer at any time. Upon the death of the owner, the property goes to the owner's designated heirs. Also known as fee absolute.

Fifteen-year mortgage

A loan with a term of 15 years. Although the monthly payment on a 15-year mortgage is higher than that of a 30-year mortgage, the amount of interest paid over the life of the loan is substantially less.

Fixed-rate mortgage

A mortgage whose rate remains constant throughout the life of the mortgage.

Flood insurance

The Federal Flood Disaster Protection Act of 1973 requires that federally-regulated lenders determine if real estate to be used to secure a loan is located in a Specially Flood Hazard Area (SFHA). If the property is located in a SFHA area, the borrower must obtain and maintain flood insurance on the property. Most insurance agents can assist in obtaining flood insurance.

G

Gift

This includes amounts from a relative or a grant from the borrower's employer, a municipality, non-profit religious organization, or non-profit community organization that does not have to be repaid.

Ginnie Mae

Nickname for Government National Mortgage Association (GNMA).

Good faith estimate

Estimate on closing costs and monthly mortgage payments provided by the lender to the homebuyer within 3 days of applying for a loan.

Government National Mortgage Association (GNMA or Ginnie Mae)

A government organization that participates in the secondary market, securitizing pools of FHA, VA, and RHS loans.

H

Hazard insurance

A form of insurance that protects the insured property against physical damage such as fire and tornadoes. Mortgage lenders often require a borrower to maintain an amount of hazard insurance on the property that is equal at least to the amount of the mortgage loan.

Home equity loan

A mortgage on the borrower's principal residence, usually for the purpose of making home improvements or debt consolidation.

Home Inspection

A thorough review of the physical aspects and condition of a home by a professional home inspector. This inspection should be completed prior to closing so that any repairs or changes can be completed before the home is sold.

Homeowners Association (HOA)

Organization of the homeowners in a particular Subdivision, planned unit development, or Condominium. It is generally formed for the purpose of enforcing deed restrictions or managing the Common Elements of the development

Homeowners insurance

A form of insurance that protects the insured property against loss from theft, liability and most common disasters, called Hazard Insurance by the lender.

Housing and Urban Development. (HUD)

The U.S. government agency that administers FHA, GNMA and other housing programs.

Housing affordability index

Indicates what proportion of homebuyers can afford to buy an average-priced home in specified areas. The most well known housing affordability index is published by the National Association of Realtors.

I
Income approach to value

A method used by real estate appraisers to predict a property's anticipated future income. Income property includes shopping centers, hotels, motels, restaurants, apartment buildings, office space and so forth.

Index

A published interest rate compiled from other indicators such as U.S. Treasury bills or the monthly average interest rate on loans closed by savings and loan organizations. Mortgage lenders use the index figure to establish rates on adjustable rate mortgages (ARMs).

Insurance

As a part of PITI, the amount of the monthly mortgage payment that does not include the principal, interest, and taxes.

Interest

The amount of the entire mortgage loan which does not include the principal. Also, as a part of PITI, the amount of the monthly mortgage payment which does not include the principal, taxes, and insurance.

Interest rate

The simple interest rate, stated as a percentage, charged by a lender on the principal amount of borrowed money.

J
Jumbo loan

A nonconforming loan that is larger than the limits set by the Federal National Mortgage Association (FNMA) or Federal Home Loan Mortgage Corporation (FHLMC) guidelines.

L
Lien
A claim against a property for the payment of a debt. A mortgage is a lien; other types of liens a property might have include a tax lien for overdue taxes or a mechanics lien for unpaid debt to a subcontractor.

Liquidity
The capability of an asset to be readily converted into cash.

Loan Originator
A person that is licensed to take loan applications and originate mortgage loans for borrowers. The loan originator is the only one licensed to discuss rates and terms of the loan with a borrower.

Loan-to-value ratio (LTV)
The relationship, expressed as a percentage, between the amount of the proposed loan and a property's appraised value. For example, a $75,000 loan on a property appraised at $100,000 is a 75% loan-to-value.

Lock-in:
The guarantee of a specific interest rate and/or points for a specific period of time. Some lenders will charge a fee for locking in an interest rate.

M
Maintenance costs
The cost of the upkeep of the house. These costs may be minor in cost and nature (replacing washers in the faucets) or major in cost and nature (new heating system or a new roof) and can apply to either the interior or exterior of the house.

Margin
The amount a lender adds to the index of an adjustable rate mortgage to establish an adjusted interest rate. For

example, a margin of 1.50 added to a 7 percent index establishes an adjusted interest rate of 8.50 percent.

Market value

The price a property can realistically sell for, based upon comparable selling prices of other properties in the same area.

Modification

A change in the terms of the mortgage note, such as a reduction in the interest rate or change in maturity date.

Mortgage

A legal instrument in which property serves as security for the repayment of a loan. In some states, a deed of trust is used rather than a mortgage.

Mortgage banker

A lender that originates, closes, services and sells mortgage loans to the secondary

Mortgage broker

An intermediary between a borrower and a lender. A broker's expertise is to help borrowers find financing that they might not otherwise find themselves.

Mortgage insurance

Money paid to insure the lender against loss due to foreclosure or loan default. Mortgage insurance is required on conventional loans with less than a 20 percent down payment. FHA mortgage insurance requires a payment of 1.5 percent of the loan amount to be paid at closing, as well as an annual fee of 0.5 percent of the loan amount added to each monthly payment.

Mortgage interest

Interest rate charge for borrowing the money for the mortgage. It is a used to calculate the interest payment on the mortgage each month.

Mortgage term

The length of time that a mortgage is scheduled to exist. Example: a 30-year mortgage term is for 30 years.

Mortgagee

The lender.

Mortgagor

The borrower.

N

Negative amortization

A situation in which a borrower is paying less interest than what is actually being charged for a mortgage loan. The unpaid interest is added to the loan's principal. The borrower may end up owing more than the original amount of the mortgage.

Non-assumption clause

In a mortgage contract, a statement that prohibits a new buyer from assuming a mortgage loan without the approval of the lender.

Non-conforming loan

A loan that does not conform to Federal National Mortgage Association (FNMA) or Federal Home Loan Mortgage Corporation (FHLMC) guidelines. Jumbo loans are nonconforming. See also: conforming loan.

Note

A signed document that acknowledges a debt and shows the borrower is obligated to pay it.

Notice of Value (NOV)

The value of the property as determined by VA or VA approved lender based on the appraisal for a VA loan.

O

Open-end mortgage

A mortgage allowing the borrower to receive advances of principal from the lender during the life of the loan.

Origination fee

The amount charged by a lender to originate and close a mortgage loan. Origination fees are usually expressed in points.

P

P&I

Abbreviation for principal and interest.

PITI

Abbreviation for principal, interest, taxes and insurance.

Points

Charges levied by the lender based on the loan amount. Each point equals one percent of the loan amount; for example, two points on a $100,000 mortgage is $2,000. Discount points are used to buy down the interest rate. Points can also include a loan origination fee, which is usually one point.

Pre-qualification

Tentative establishment of a borrower's qualification for a mortgage loan amount of a specific range, based on the borrower's assets, debts, and income.

Prime rate

The interest rate commercial banks charge their most creditworthy customers.

Principal

The amount of the entire mortgage loan, not counting interest. Also, as a part of PITI, the amount of the monthly mortgage payment which does not include the interest, insurance, and taxes.

Property tax

The amount which the state and/or locality assesses as a tax on a piece of property.

Prorate

To proportionally divide amounts owed by the buyer and the seller at closing.

Q

Qualification

As determined by a lender, the ability of the borrower to repay a mortgage loan based on the borrower's credit history, employment history, assets, debts and income.

R
RESPA
Abbreviation for the Real Estate Settlement Procedures Act, which allows consumers to review settlement costs at application and once again prior to closing.

Reverse annuity mortgage
A type of mortgage loan in which the lender makes periodic payments to the borrower. The borrower's equity in the home is used as security for the loan.

Right of first refusal
Purchasing a property under conditions and terms made by another buyer and accepted by the seller.

Right of rescission
When a borrower's principal dwelling is going to secure a loan, the borrower has three business days following signing of the loan documents to rescind or cancel the transaction. Any and all money paid by the borrower must be refunded upon rescission. The right to rescind does not apply to loans to purchase real estate or to refinance a loan under the same terms and conditions where no additional funds will be added to the existing loan.

Rural Development (RD)
An agency which runs programs intended to improve the economy and quality of life in rural America. It oversees the USDA rural development loan program.

S
Second mortgage
A loan that is junior to a primary or first mortgage and often has a higher interest rate and a shorter term.

Secondary market
A market comprising investors like GNMA, FHLMC and FNMA, which buy large numbers of mortgages from the primary lenders and sell them to other investors.

Servicing

The responsibility of collecting monthly mortgage payments and properly crediting them to the principal, taxes and insurance, as well as keeping the borrower informed of any changes in the status of the loan.

Survey

A physical measurement of property done by a registered professional showing the dimensions and location of any buildings as well as easements, rights of way, roads, etc.

T

Tax deed

A written document conveying title to property repossessed by the government due to default on tax payments.

Tax savings

The amount of money that the homeowner is not required to pay the government in taxes because he or she owns a home.

Taxes

As a part of PITI, the amount of the monthly mortgage payment which does not include the principal, interest, and insurance.

Tenancy

Joint tenancy - equal ownership of property by two or more parties, each with the right

of survivorship.

Tenancy by the entireties - ownership of property only between husband and wife in

which neither can sell without the consent of the other and the property is owned by the

survivor in the event of death of either party.

Tenancy in common - equal ownership of property by two or more parties without the

right of survivorship.

Tenancy in severalty - ownership of property by one legal entity or a sole party.

Tenancy at will - a license to use or occupy a property at the will of the owner.

Title

A formal document establishing ownership of property.

Title insurance

A policy issued by a title insurance company insuring the purchaser against any errors in the title search. The cost of title insurance may be paid for by the buyer, the seller or both.

Truth in Lending Act

The Truth in Lending Act requires lenders to disclose the Annual Percentage Rate and other associated costs to homebuyers within three working days of the loan application.

U

Underwriter

A professional who approves or denies a loan to a potential homebuyer based on the homebuyer's credit history, employment history, assets, debts and other factors such as loan guidelines.

Uniform Settlement Statement

A standard document prescribed by the Real Estate Settlement Procedures Act containing information for closing which must be supplied to both buyer and seller.

Utility costs

Periodic housing costs for water, electricity, natural gas, heating oil, etc.

V

Veterans Administration (VA)

The federal agency responsible for the VA loan guarantee program as well as other services for eligible veterans. In general, qualified veterans can apply for home loans with no down payment and a funding fee of 1 percent of the loan amount.

W
walk-through
An inspection of a property by the prospective buyer prior to closing on a mortgage.
warranty deed
A document protecting a homebuyer against any and all claims to the property.

Y
yield
The rate of earnings from an investment.

Z
zoning
The ability of local governments to specify the use of private property in order to control development within designated areas of land. For example, some areas of a neighborhood may be designated only for residential use and others for commercial use such as stores, gas stations, etc.

Index